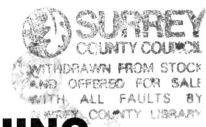
POLE FISHING

Wayne Swinscoe
and
Don Slaymaker

Compiled and edited by Dave King

Beekay Publishers

Other angling titles by Beekay Publishers:

Coarse

Carp Fever by Kevin Maddocks
The Art of Pole Fishing by Dickie Carr
Pike Fishing in the 80's by Neville Fickling
Basic Carp Fishing by Peter Mohan
Modern Specimen Hunting by Jim Gibbinson
Top Ten – tactics for the major species from ten leading anglers
Edited by Bruce Vaughan
Redmire Pool by Kevin Clifford & Len Arbery
Tactics for Big Pike by Bill Chillingworth
In Pursuit of Carp & Catfish by Kevin Maddocks
Cypry The Carp by Peter Mohan
The Beekay Guide to 450 Carp Waters
Jim Davidson Gets Hooked by Jim Davidson
In Pursuit of Predatory Fish by Neville Fickling
Tiger Bay by Rob Maylin
Understanding Barbel by Fred Crouch
Big-Water Carp by Jim Gibbinson
Mega-Pike by Eddie Turner

Sea

Boat Fishing at Sea by Phill Williams & Brian Douglas
Long Range Casting & Fishing Techniques by Paul Kerry
Cod Fishing by John Rawle
Uptide & Boatcasting by Bob Cox

Game

The Colour Guide to Fly Tying by Kevin Hyatt
Robson's Guide to Stillwater Trout Flies by Kenneth Robson
Dressed to Kill by Bob Carnill & Kenneth Robson

First published in 1990 by
BEEKAY PUBLISHERS
WITHY POOL, BEDFORD ROAD,
HENLOW CAMP, BEDS. SG16 6EA

ISBN 0 947674 34 9

Typeset by BP Integraphics Ltd., Bath, Avon
Printed in Breat Britain at The Bath Press, Avon

Contents

Introduction

By Dave King

'When fishing on still or flowing water, where the fish can be brought within range, modern poles in the hands of accomplished anglers make rods and reels redundant in most match fishing situations within a radius of 8 metres of the peg'.

When I made this then controversial statement at my local Association's National Squad meeting in 1976 I was almost lynched. The comments I received are unprintable. Now in 1990 no one will dispute this statement except for the range, which has now been increased to 14 metres due to the development of ever longer and lighter poles. Due to its simplicity anyone can easily catch fish on a pole providing full advantage is taken of the fineness of the tackle that the method allows. So why is it that the same small group of anglers who always used to win regularly with the running line are now repeating their monopoly of the prize money by using the pole?

The methods themselves are not necessarily the key, but the way these anglers make the methods work is, backed by a self confidence that is lacking in many of us and coupled with a vast range of experience gathered over many years of fishing a wide range of venues and methods and taking success for granted.

A glimpse into the tackle boxes of top anglers such as Wayne and Don is quite revealing. Instead of the expected wide range of floats and tackles neatly laid out in a regimented order, all made up and suited for the infinite and slight variations thrown up under various conditions, just a half dozen winders and a handful of floats that have seen better days are all that meet the eye. Next to them is a small bundle of hook packets containing a few different hook sizes and patterns and a couple of spools of line for the hooklengths and alongside a handful of mixed split shot and Styl leads, which made up the balance of their terminal tackle requirements. As you may have gathered by now, simplicity is another key to their success.

The other important factor is the feeding. They seem to know instinctively when or when not to use groundbait and a number of lines will be continually fed throughout the match and they know exactly when to change from one to the other and when to increase or decrease the rate at which they feed. All tackle handling functions are carried out smoothly and efficiently, with a deceptive, unhurried speed, and the tackle and bait are in the water for the maximum period possible throughout the match. Yes, pole fishing is simple, and these lads make it look even easier. Watching them fire out a pouchful of loose feed or throw out a ball of groundbait into an area the size of a bucket top whilst hanging on to 11 metres of pole looks very easy until you try it. The truth is of course that it takes a lot of practice to do it properly, without conscious thought, and if more anglers concentrated more on mastering these 'little things' instead of working out more and more complicated rigs and float patterns, I am certain that they would improve upon their overall results in real terms.

When I took on the commission to write this series of books and the Shakespeare Superteam agreed to these no holds barred interviews, I knew I had the chance to produce something really special. I was determined on behalf of myself and the other 90% of lesser mortals not to blow it and not to come away with a missed opportunity. As to the final result only you, the reader, can judge.

I feel that by keeping the interviews in the format of how they actually went, as opposed to re-hashing them into normal book form, I have kept the authoratitive sincerity of the anglers concerned with regard to both content and fact. If your overall approach is transformed as much as mine has been after reading it, then I feel I will have succeeded.

Best wishes and tight lines.

Profile: Wayne Swinscoe

Wayne started fishing at the age of 8. His father, who was a non angler, took him to Clumber Park lake three times but he never caught a fish. Undaunted, he pestered his dad to take him somewhere decent and a couple of his father's workmates took him with them to the Upper Welland where not only could he see the fish but he could catch a few as well.

During the school holidays he used to fish his local ponds and a few years later he joined his father's works fishing club. He used to do his morning paper round and finish in time to catch the club bus. Most of the trips went out to the Ouse and Fens and he really enjoyed these outings and after a few years he started to win the odd match.

After he left school he went pleasure fishing on Saturdays and on club matches with his mates, a few of whom he still goes fishing with now. They concentrated mainly on the Fenland venues as at that time the Trent was fishing very poorly, and the Fens offered the best sport.

After a few years, at the age of 17 he teamed up with Frank Barlow, Gerry Woodcock, Terry Dorman and a few other local Nottingham lads and started to fish the odd Sunday open match on the river Trent which by now was beginning to show some form, but did no good at all, so he drifted back into club fishing to restore his confidence.

A season or so later he again tried his luck on the open circuit and began to win the odd section; it was all caster fishing in those days and no one had yet heard of a Leeds angler called Dave Thomas. Wayne was still getting a right hammering on occasions, but he gradually got the caster method cracked, winning five good matches of 100 pegs plus including the Tom Draper Memorial and the Doncaster Hospitals Cup at Dunham Bridge. Just as he had got the caster method sorted out it all changed around. Dave Thomas came on to the scene and the whole river switched over the bronze maggot. He was very loath to change and stuck with the caster for another season, gradually going downhill, but after seeing Dave Thomas beat his caster fishing hero Pete Warren off adjacent pegs he thought, 'Right, maggots here we go' and left the casters and his beloved centrepin at home.

After a bit he got it sorted out and started to win again and branched out once more to the Fens which by this time were predominantly roach waters, and as most of the locals were still persevering with the caster, he and his Trentmen friends who had now been joined by Don, started to clean up. They also started travelling down to the Thames and the Bristol Avon which they found to be easy fishing and again had a lot of success.

Eventually they started to fish the Birmingham Parks matches, also doing well and it was at this time that the late Clive Smith stepped in and invited Wayne, Don and Frank Barlow to join the Shakespeare Superteam.

At that time they had between them won everything on the Trentmen scene and had found that they were not progressing, so they jumped at the opportunity, and in the last few years Wayne has learnt a lot about all the various aspects of match fishing and really enjoys it. The travelling gets him down at times but he feels this is more than compensated for by being about to fish at the highest level, but even so, he still enjoys his midweek knock ups on his local Trent when his team calendar allows, keeping in touch with his old friends and occasionally being brought back to earth.

Profile: Don Slaymaker

Don also started fishing at eight years old; his grandad first took him with him when he went livebait fishing to a local lake in Stoke on Trent. He gave him a go on his rod and Don caught his first of many gudgeon and that was it, he was hooked. His dad, who was a non-angler saw that he was keen and so he bought him some tackle and took him out during school holidays.

He then joined his first club, Stoke City and District, and started fishing the local canals using the bread punch and small maggot baits, and it was here that he first met a few of the top Lancashire lads including Benny Ashurst and Ginger Pennington. He was mesmerised by watching them fish and he tried to copy them but unfortunately did not do it very well.

Eventually he began to work out his own style. He started to compete in a few club matches but did not do any good as it was a big club with a large keen membership and as a novice he stood little chance. At the age of 13 he joined a small club that had a large reservoir, Stanley Pool A.C. and they ran juvenile matches on the lake and Don won the very first one that he entered with 5 lbs of perch. All he wanted to do after that was to fish all of the juvenile matches around Stoke on Trent and he did quite well. He won a couple more and some nice trophies which he still treasures to this day.

Then he left school and although he still went fishing, he concentrated his main efforts on his Joiners Apprenticeship and just went fishing at weekends. After a few years, fishing again took over as his main interest but then had to take a back seat when he met his future wife. After they were married they moved down to Cornwall and there was none of the type of fishing that Don was used to. His wife's aunt who lived at Nottingham used to send them the Evening Post down every week and Don would read these, particularly the Thursday Edition which contained the local match results, and this decided him to move and go and live in Nottingham. So they moved up and Don started walking the banks of the Trent and watching the local cracks. Eventually he got talking to a few of them and decided that he really wanted to master fishing the river.

Luckily he met a few lads from the Raleigh fishing club and he joined them and then it was match fishing every weekend, and he really got into the local match fishing scene. He won a few matches and shortly afterwards the Trentman Club was formed and he thought it was one of the best things to happen for anglers in Nottingham. It was formed especially for local anglers who wanted to fish the Nottingham Open Circuit. At about this time he started to fish Steve Toone's Saturday matches and he will never forget his good fortune in winning the first 3 that he fished. After a few years and a number of notable successes later he was invited along with Wayne and Frank Barlow to join the Shakespeare Superteam and he says that this was the greatest thing ever to happen to him. He feels very privileged to be fishing for such a top class outfit and enjoys the challenge immensely.

The Shakespeare Superteam

The name 'The Shakespeare Superteam' needs very little introduction to anyone who knows and partakes in the sport of match fishing. Since their formation they have always been the team to beat if success is to be assured and have always been at the forefront of angling acheivement. Their consistency has always been based upon having the cream of current angling talent in their ranks, and this being encouraged and directed to its full potential by the team manager and Captain Ken Giles. The strength of the team lies in the fact that it consists of a strong and resolute core of individual anglers. This may sound like a contradiction in terms, but Ken is certain that this quality of individualism is what makes them so consistent as a team. Their general allround ability, combined with their individual approach to the various methods required to be utilised under a variety of conditions, is what makes up their awesome collective strength. Over the years, names have changed and new talent has been brought forward and encouraged, ensuring a continuity in results virtually unequalled in match fishing history. Team championships and competitions are a development of the last decade and will be at the forefront of angling in the future, whatever that future may bring. The days of the secretive individual were numbered once the format of the old 'All England Championships' was altered from an individual and team weight, to a team points system. Professionalism has now taken over and no team typifies this approach more than the Superteam.

Under the banner of Glevum A.C. they have risen through each of the divisions annually to achieve their rightful place in Division one of the N.F.A. Championships and it is only a matter of time before the title of Division One Champions is assured.

I will now let Ken take over and tell the story of the teams conception and what he considers to be the key to its success.

Ken: In 1973, Clive Smith and I approached various tackle companies with a view to financial sponsorship. At that time this had never been done before and was a totally new concept with regard to angling. A few top anglers had, in the past, associated themselves with tackle companies and put their names to various products, but no-one had approached anyone with regard to actual cash sponsorship to represent the company on the match circuit.

Most of them laughed us off and said that this sort of thing can never happen, but one company, Shakespeare, did not dismiss us out of hand. We had a couple of meetings with them and they did show some interest. They saw that Clive and I were getting fairly consistent results and they saw that there could be something in it for the benefit of the promotion of the company and, of course, for Clive and myself.

In the end they decided to sponsor us and in return we were given a free hand in the development and design of specific products for the match angler and these became very successful. The Match International range of rods and reels became very popular and out-sold any other company's match fishing products during this period.

Up to this time, major angling matches and events were tailored to individual weight performance and what few team events there were also concentrated on total weight to decide the outcome. Apart from the National Championships, these were mainly aimed at four-man teams, and would run a four-man team prize as a supplement to the major prize which was aimed at individual performance. Again these would be decided on a total weight basis, but each man would draw as an individual. At this time there were no sectional draws for the team event.

To try to make our mark under the system as it stood, we were allowed to recruit two more members into the sponsorship arrangement with a view to entering the team events. These two were Max Winters and Tony Davis. This lasted for several years and we were quite successful as both a team and as individuals.

Eventually, due to the increased interest and publicity generated by the success of ourselves and other teams such as the Leicester Likely Lads and the Starlets etc., team events became more popular and in some top events these were expanded for teams of six. To be able to take part in these and also to give ourselves a pool from which to field a four-man team regardless of illness, holidays etc., we recruited another two anglers:- Dave Williams and Steve Webb.

Currently, only three of the original six are still fishing. As most people know, Clive, sadly died, and Max Winters and Dave Williams have both given up fishing totally. This was a great loss to angling, but unfortunately these things inevitably happen.

By this time, team fishing as we know it now, was rapidly being developed. The introduction of the points system in the National Championships was adopted for the winter and summer league events and many of these now catered for teams of up to twelve anglers. Due to the success we had achieved, and the effect this had on tackle development and sales, the Shakespeare Company allowed us to expand our squad to its present level of fourteen anglers, from which a strong team of twelve can be selected at any one time, with regard to current form and strengths on each particular venue. It also helps with things such as holidays and work commitments, occasional health or family problems etc. If we only had twelve members and due to a car breaking down or sudden illness we were a man short on the day, as a team we would be dead. So by having a squad of fourteen we can always be certain, in a twelve-man event, of fielding a strong team.

There have been a number of changes over the years. For various reasons anglers have lost form, or due to working or matrimonial pressures, have been unable to maintain their commitment to the sport and it is my job as Captain and Manager to maintain the continuity and strength within the squad. All the squad members are very experienced, successful individual anglers within their own right, but when we fish as a team they are committed team anglers.

The selection of the team on the day is my decision alone. None of the team is consulted or needs to be concerned with team selection. There are times when I have the unpleasant job of telling a team member he is dropped, due to lack of form etc., but my decision is always unquestionably accepted and with good spirit. This policy is, I feel, the best for the morale of the team in the long term. I do not agree with systems where teams are decided by selection of a committee or by consultation. If that same enthusiasm was shown on the river bank as is shown around a bar when discussing and selecting team members, these teams would win everything going. Instead I think they are negative and divisive.

Such is our relationship and commitment that I rarely have to make the decision to drop an angler for a particular match. If, due to loss of form or any other reason, any of the lads feels he should be dropped for a particular match, he will normally approach me with this view in mind, as opposed to me approaching him. Should this happen, I know I can still count upon him turning up on the day, if asked, to run the bank and give us 110% effort in collating and passing on the necessary information to the team.

One of our greatest strengths is that our team consists of a majority of mature anglers who are settled in their life-styles and have the full support of their families and employers. This is essential if you are to give the degree of commitment necessary to succeed. Many anglers can do this over a period of two or three years, but to maintain this over a period of ten or twelve years, despite the pitfalls that they will inevitably come up against, means that these men are exceptional. They are something special and I am proud to have anglers of this calibre in the team. They are the key to our continual success.

About The Pole

Q. *The 1980's was the boom decade as far as pole fishing is concerned, with everyone from tackle manufactures to anglers jumping onto the bandwagon. Several seasons ago if you walked along the banks of the River Trent, one man in a hundred would be using a pole and most people would have thought he was mad. Now on any top class river match, many anglers will have one or two poles set up. As two of the most respected running line anglers in the country, why has this come about, and what has convinced you that the pole now has its place as a potential winner on flowing as well as still water?.*

Wayne: When poles first started to appear on the general match scene in the mid seventies we were very sceptical about them and considered them to be just another passing fad. At that time they were made of fibre glass and due to the weight of the material the maximum length was only 7 or 8 metres. I did try one out and I did catch fish on it, but it seemed a very clumsy and awkward tool to use and as I was having a lot of success at that time on the running line and all of the matches I was fishing were being won on the running line, I discounted it as a viable method. It was only when I started to go over to Ireland during the closed season and saw how devastating the method could be due to the nature of the fishing over there, that I started to look at its potential seriously, but then it was only in the context of its application in Ireland where vast numbers of fish could be caught at 5 or 6 metres out, using heavy lines, big floats and big hooks.

After a few seasons had passed I had got used to using a pole in this situation and also the carbon poles began to appear on the scene which were much thinner and lighter than the glass poles, which made them easier to handle, particularly in windy conditions. So it gradually became apparent that the method could be used to our advantage on English rivers under certain situations where the fish could be brought up to within pole range. So we started to experiment by using traditional stick floats and shotting patterns, as at that time (in the late 70's) the types of pole floats that we now take for granted were unobtainable.

These experiments did meet with limited success, but unlike in Ireland, it was seldom that the larger species could be brought to within pole range and although you could catch lots of small fish on the method, as a match winner it was still a non-starter if the bigger fish were feeding, as these were being caught on the waggler, which was the match winning method at that time.

It was around 1982–83 that a number of important changes came about, and which allowed us to consider looking into the use of the pole again.

The technology had taken a big leap foward and poles had become longer, stiffer and lighter, increasing the range at which you could fish with them effectively. The terminal tackle had also been greatly improved and a good range of floats, Olivettes and Styl leads had become more readily available. Matches were still being won mainly on the running line on the rivers, but the pole was also being used in conjunction with normal float tactics when the fish came into range, and its use was contributing to an increasing proportion of the overall catch rate. Due to this, even the most sceptical anglers were now recognising this fact and so as more and more top class river anglers came to experiment with the pole, so the methods were developed and perfected and the pole gradually became more widely accepted as an effective weapon.

At the same time as all of this was happening the nature of the rivers was also changing, particularly the Trent. Lots of skimmer bream were appearing along the river and these were taking over from the roach and chub as the dominant species in certain areas, and pole fishing methods are particularly effective with these species. Fish populations were also on the increase generally, as was angling pressure, so as the angler needed to go even finer to get bites, so the use of the pole became an increasingly more attractive option.

Whilst we are primarily concerned with pole methods in this book, the reader must be aware that it is not an exclusive method, especially on rivers. We use the pole these days far more than ever before and pole-caught fish increasingly make up the larger proportion of our overall catch, but it is a very brave angler who only sets up a pole to fish a river. The stick float and the waggler still need to be used in conjunction with pole tactics, only using the pole when the feeding fish are brought to within pole range. Often during the course of a match the fish will move down or out of pole range and a change to the running line needs to be made to maintain the catch rate. A lot depends upon the conditions on the day and the nature of the swim, as to what part the pole is likely to contribute during the match. Wind plays a great part in this decision. In very windy conditions, even with the ultra thin poles of today, it is physically impossible to hang onto a long pole for any length of time and difficult to present the bait properly. Also on shallow fast flowing water it is also difficult to bring quality fish up to within pole range for any appreciable length of time.

Subject to reasonable conditions and a workable depth and flow, I often start on a pole to take a few quick fish which may happen to be within range, switching to the running line as these are exhausted and I need to start building up the swim in the conventional manner. Once I have brought a shoal up to within pole range I will then switch back to the pole to speed up the catch rate, changing back to the running line if the fish drop back or move out. I will still be feeding a waggler line further out whilst all of this is going on, switching to this when I feel the closer range swim requires resting.

This process will be continued throughout the match. Both lines will be continually fed and you will change from one to the other as the bite rate dictates, allowing the fish to settle down again so that when you do go back on it you can have a good session and maintain the catch rate.

The skill is knowing when to put the pole down and pick up the float rod and vice versa. Sometimes you can pick the pole up and absolutely murder them and suddenly they have gone, you then pick the stick float up to chase them about and it's sometimes even better. The reverse is also true, you think you are doing well on the stick float and then you think 'Well I'll just try the pole,' and you find you are doing twice as well. The important thing to remember when measuring your catch rate is to consider the 'weight' of fish you are catching as opposed to the number of fish.

If the fish you are catching on the pole are the same size as the fish you are catching on the stick float or waggler, and you are catching them faster, then all well and good. But if you are catching bigger fish on the float, even at a much slower rate, but the overall weight over a period of time is greater, then it will pay you to keep going on the running line whilst this level of catch rate is maintained.

The thing is to measure your performance against that of the anglers pegged around you and alter in response to way the fish are moving around.

Don: Like Wayne I first realised the potential of the pole in Ireland, but I started with it on the Trent much sooner than Wayne did. In fact, when I bought my first pole I used it in a match the following weekend and actually won it, although I must admit it was down more to good fortune at the drawbag than to my technique, as the method I used was really a standard stick float fished to hand. But the pole did allow me to present it better under the prevailing conditions and I had the fish in pole range for most of the match so my catch rate was much quicker.

At that time it was generally a small fish method and some anglers such as Kevin Ashurst were taking very big weights of gudgeon close in. Then, for some reason, these fish seemed to disappear overnight and the larger fish moved out into the centre of the river as it became much cleaner and the waggler then began to dominate the match results.

Due to my early success with the pole, I did still persevere with it during practice and as the specialist bristle floats and the rest of the pole technology began to develop, so my own development of the methods was expanded and when the opportunity to use it to my advantage presented itself I did so with increasing effect. Once I had joined the Shakespeare Superteam and I started to fish a much wider variety of venues, I learned a lot from my team mates about the pole's potential on still waters and canals, and together we developed its use on all types of waters, sharing our experiences and developing new ideas.

Eventually, due to our experience and the ever changing cycle of the rivers, the pole has now come into its own on all types of venues, and as Wayne has said, now that more and more good anglers are realising its potential, so the methods and the technology is being developed to make the use of it more and more effective. I don't want to go into too much detail on the various methods at this stage, as these will be fully outlined later on in this book, but anglers have now come to realise that whenever fish of match winning quality can be brought to within pole range, it is undoubtedly the most efficient way of catching them, proving all of the aspects of tackle balance and presentation can be mastered.

Q.   *I dont want to get too bogged down with basics, but briefly, out of the hundreds of poles now available on the market, what features to you consider are essential in choosing a good pole?*

Don: A lot depends upon the types of venues you are likely to fish the most. If like ourselves you fish a wide number of different venues from canals to rivers, then providing you can afford it you need two types of pole: A strong thick walled poled with a bit of give in it for long lining on rivers, or for when fishing for bigger fish such as in Ireland, and a lightweight stiff actioned pole for fishing the short line on still waters and canals.

On canals particularly you are generally fishing from 11 metres to 14 metres, so you do need a light-weight stiff pole, but for river fishing you seldom exceed 9 metres and a strong robust pole is needed to cope with the continual action, with enough flexibility to assist casting light tackle on a long line.

If you specialise on one particular type of venue then you must go for the type best suited to it. If you fish a variety of venues but can only afford one pole, then you need to go for the more robust type as this will cover both aspects.

Wayne: Don is right about this. You have got to look at the situation from the point of view of where you will be doing most of your fishing.

Being in the Shakespeare Superteam we seem to be here, there and everywhere, on the Avon, canals, lakes etc., plus our local venues on the Trent or on the Rowing Course at Holme Pierrepont, all calling for different types of pole with regards to the qualities that Don has mentioned. The last couple of top range poles that Shakespeare have brought out, and the new Superteam put-over pole in particular, lend themselves to most types of fishing, being good all round poles. They will cope with both jobs pretty well. Having said that, for river work I do not feel that the average angler needs to go to quite that expense, as some of the cheaper range poles are very suitable for this type of work, being generally heavier and thicker walled. When you are fishing 7 or 8 metres to hand it is very easy with a light walled pole to crunch it under the pressure of your hand squeezing it, whereas a good thick walled pole will stand this sort of hammer. Also when upshipping sections whilst long lining, the joints often get banged against the rocks behind you and a light pole will easily chip and split if this should happen.

Also, as Don has mentioned, the heavier poles do tend to be more flexible. If you are going to be using an 8 or 9 metre pole on a river, fishing to hand and catching anything from 1 oz gudgeon to 2 lb chub, you have got to have a pole that is a bit flexible to help you to cast and also to bend when you are playing a big fish. When you do catch a big fish on a river such as the Trent, they do not run very far, but they do tend to hug the bottom and take all of your elastic out to its limit, so unless the pole can bend a good bit when this happens you will have nothing to play the fish against. Also, this bend will help you to 'feel' the fish better, letting you know when you are getting close to breaking point.

The very expensive light stiff poles now available are ideal for canal and still water work where short line tactics and very long pole lengths are normally employed. They are designed specifically for this type of work and are an essential consideration for any angler specialising in this type of fishing. The modern trend is also for poles with 'put over' joints, where the top of the larger section fits into the bottom of the smaller section. This makes the constant but necessary job of putting together and unshipping of the joints much easier. For long lining this is less of a consideration as far fewer joints are taken apart. Also the thinner diameter in ratio to the length of pole normally associated with 'put in' poles makes the general handling much easier. The slower taper also provides the extra action which as we have discussed is also essential when long lining.

Don: Many anglers these days, and quite wrongly in my opinion, are over-preoccupied with stiffness. They seem to dismiss out of hand any pole that shows the slightest tendency to droop when put together at 11 metres plus. I often have a chuckle to myself when I overhear them talking at the tackle exhibitions. Currently the trend on the Continent is to go for softer actioned poles these days. Stiffness is now out of fashion over there, which, let's face it, is the historical home of pole fishing. Ultra stiff poles are now considered to be the 'British Disease'. If the top Continental anglers are now switching to softer actioned poles, then there must be a good reason for it and I feel that it is only a matter of time before the reason for this becomes more apparent over here and the action of our poles will be more considered, as opposed to following a slavish fashion trend for stiffness. Many top British pole anglers who fish a variety of venues are now arming themselves with both types of pole, recognising the virtues of both in various situations. I only hope we have been helpful in guiding you through the maze. Buying a pole these days is a very big investment at several hundred pounds to over £1,000.00, so it is important to know that you are getting the right one for the right job.

Line And Hooks

Q. *We all have preferences in the brands and types of line we use for various types of fishing, but what qualities do you look for in lines for pole fishing and how do they differ from the types you use with the running line? What breaking strains do you use for your main lines and hooklengths?*

Wayne: The main advantage of pole fishing is that it allows the use of finer lines and smaller hooks for superior bait presentation, with less chance of being broken by good fish due to the correct use of the various grades of elastic. So it follows that you should use the finest, strongest line that is available. Up to a few years ago this meant using standard monofilament line in its finest sizes, which were classified by breaking strain. Although ½ lb line was available, ¾ lb was the normal size used. In the mid 1980's the new pre-stretched monofilament and copolyamide lines came on to the market, offering lower line diameters for the equivalent breaking strain of monofilament lines and were known as super strength or double strength lines. In the finer sizes they were next to useless for using with the running line, as they had little or no stretch and it was very easy to crack off on the strike. Despite this handicap, many pole anglers, ourselves included, saw the benefits of the lower line diameter, and as the lack of stretch could be compensated for to some degree with the elastic system of the pole, we did find them very good for pole fishing use. Having said that, you needed to be very careful when whipping up your hooks or joining the line as it was very easily damaged and weakened at these points.

As with many aspects of pole fishing, technology has progressed and there are now very fine diameter lines available that have a reasonable degree of stretch, high knot strength and they are also less prone to damage where they are pulled through on the knot or on the whip when tying hooks.

Two brands that I use are Tubertini and Tectan. They are very expensive, but for pole use, as they are not subjected to the wear or friction associated with lines used with a rod and reel, they last a very long time and a single spool will keep you going all season. As you would expect

Two examples of modern 'superlines' ideal for pole fishing use, note that they are classified by diameter in fractions of a millimeter

with an expensive line they are of a very high quality, very soft and supple. You can tell the quality when you tie your hooks to them, there are no shiny bits occurring where the line is pulled through the whip which normally indicates slight damage and weakness.

I used to use standard monofilament lines for my main lines and Tectan for my hook lengths, but this season, after talking to Bob Nudd and a few other top pole anglers, I have swapped over to using it for main lines as well. Normally I use 0.08 mm for the main line and 0.06 mm for my hooklengths and I find it gives me a lot better control over my float, especially when it's windy, as the wind does not seem to affect it as much as it did with the thicker monofilament. 0.08 mm Tectan is the same diameter as 1 lb mono' but is rated at about 1.8 lb breaking strain.

Don: The line manufacturers are getting line right now. They are producing much finer lines for a given breaking strain, with the important qualities of softness, high stretch and resistance to damage by friction. These latter qualities were lacking in the earlier attempts at producing the so called double strength or super lines. As Wayne has said, they are expensive, but match anglers are prepared to invest extra money for quality, especially when it means he can put more fish into the net. In any competitive sport, no participant can afford to ignore products that give a definite advantage, and these new lines do give you that.

Having said that, they cannot take over from standard monofilament for general use as they cannot take the hammer that the rod rings and the reel bail arm gives them. They are too thin and soft to be practical under these circumstances, but for pole use they are ideal. By being fine and soft they allow the hookbait to act far more naturally, and by being clear they are also visibly undetectable.

The trend now is to use much shorter hooklengths to reduce the amount of shot used on the hooklength. This makes re-tackling after a breakage much quicker and reduces the chances of line damage caused by putting shot on the line in the first place. With the earlier superlines that had little or no stretch this was always a problem, as a long length had to be used to help cushion the shock and prevent cracking off when you struck into a fish. Now that a reasonable degree of stretch is built in, much shorter hooklengths can be used. As Wayne has stated, the use of a pole does give you far superior presentation, even when used with traditional lines, so the advantages of these new lines can only enhance this and produce far more bites.

Wayne: Yes, being able to use shorter hooklengths is a definite advantage, particularly when fishing on flowing water, where often you are picking up snags as your tackle goes through the swim. It does usually ensure that as your olivette is well up on the main line, if you do have to pull for a break, only the hooklength is lost and not an expensive olivette. Also, by having most of the shot or Style leads on the main line, it only takes a few seconds to replace the hooklengths and get back into the water as quickly as possible. The maximum length I use now on the pole is about six inches. This means that providing I balance this to a stronger main line, if I do snag up I will only loose the hooklength and perhaps one shot, as often on the Trent and other rivers you do still need to have at least one shot very close to the hook. On still waters this is less of a problem and normally all of my shot will be on the main line. Having said that, it is very rare that you ever get snagged up on still waters or canals, so you seldom need to replace the hooklength, except when changing your hook type or size. I always try to maintain an 0.02 mm differential between my mainline and hooklength to ensure that I will always break off at the hooklength if I get snagged. If you go too close, say 0.07 mm mainline to 0.06 mm hooklength, then due to the possibility of weakening the main line whilst moving shots about, there is a greater risk of breaking off higher up on the main line. By going up to 0.08 mm, this risk is minimised and so far I have not experienced any problems with this degree of balance.

The one exception to this is if a shoal of big fish such as chub or bream move in. Providing your swim is snag free, you can then tie your hook directly to the 0.08 mm main line to give you the extra power to get them out quickly without the risk of breaking. To save time in these circumstances I would take off my thinner hooklength, move the float and the olivette up to compensate for the loss of depth and tie a larger hook, if I think I can get away with it, directly onto the main line.

It is important when match fishing to capitalise on these sudden changes in circumstances, and be able to react swiftly and positively, making the most of your good fortune.

Q. *What hook patterns and sizes do you use when pole fishing for the various baits and species and how would these differ for use on canals or rivers?.*

Wayne: Again this comes down to fineness and balance to achieve the best possible bait presentation. Fortunately, hook technology has kept abreast of line technology. Hooks of a given size and strength are now being made in lighter, finer wire, enabling the angler to complement the finer, stronger lines that are now available. I have just mentioned the importance of using a larger, stronger hook in conjunction with a stepped up line strength when a shoal of big, hungry fish move in, but this situation is the exception rather than the rule, so under most circumstances the priority is to induce as many bites as possible by using the best means of presentation. This is achieved by using the finest lines and the lightest hooks that conditions will allow.

The traditional use of Mustad 90340, or Whisker barbs since the chub population has declined a bit, still has its place on the running line, but for pole fishing with the new fine 0.06 mm hooklengths you need to go even finer.

These last couple of years I have changed over to the Tubertini Series 2 or 8 for still water and canal work, and for river fishing I now use the D.A.M. Gamakatsu 6315 Silver Microbarb hooks. These are a semi-round bend pattern which I think helps. For some reason I do not seem to lose so many fish on these.

They are quite strong but they are very, very fine and they penetrate really well. They also have a fairly wide gape on them but this seems to help the hooking and holding power. I have been using them from size 18 to 24 and have had no problems with them at all. I have held on to big chub on the Avon with them thinking 'this is going to go', but they have held in and been successfully landed. Now I would not use anything else with caster and maggot whilst river fishing with the pole unless I knew I was going to get into some really big fish. Then I would use something like a forged Kamasan B920, but I would increase the strength of my hooklength to match it anyway.

For maggot and caster fishing on canal and still water venues, where I know I am unlikely to encounter bigger fish, I will use the Gamakatsu 6311 blue wire hooks. These are finer wire still to the silver ones and obviously not as strong, but the weight saving is the important consideration, and as I am only catching small fish anyway, they are still up to this particular job.

It is important when using these very fine wire hooks to use a disgorger to remove them. This reduces the risk of bending them out of shape during the unhooking process. For bloodworm or squatt fishing on the pole I use the size 24 Drennan carbon caster hooks, the blue ones, or if I need something a bit stronger, the Tubertini Series 2's.

The Drennan caster hooks are very good and are unbeatable as squatt hooks for small fish; again, care needs to be taken when unhooking as the shanks are prone to bending unless a disgorger is used, but the advantage of the superior presentation far outweights this inconvenience.

When fishing in Ireland we go completely the other way. With this type of fishing you need big strong hooks which allow you to swing in really big fish. For this type of work we use the Geoffrey Bucknall fly hooks, size 12 or 14. This may sound crude but these really are the business for these big bagging sessions. The wire is really strong and the upturned eye stops the bait from being blown up the line, a big time saver.

Don: Like most items of tackle, the choice of hook is a very personal thing and what suits one angler does not always suit another. All we can do in this book is tell the reader what we use and why, and then it is up to them to try them out if they wish to and arrive at their own conclusions.

There are those days when the fish will take the bait regardless, within reason, of the size or type of hook. But with the ever increasing angling pressure on most match venues we find that on many occasions we have to put a lot more consideration into our choice of terminal tackle and need to take advantage of the latest changes in technology to maintain a reasonable catch rate or advantage. The hook is the most important item of tackle and most anglers now appreciate that it is the weight rather than the size of the hook which is the important consideration with regard to presentation of the bait, with strength and penetration being the important consideration once the fish has been hooked. With the hook patterns Wayne has mentioned you do have a good balance of these essential features and we have arrived at this choice with a lot of experience, over a wide number of venues and situations.

Our choice of hook pattern for float fishing or feeder fishing with the running line does vary from the types used when pole fishing, although some of the patterns are now also being successfully adopted into these branches of the sport, but the main consideration here is what we use for pole fishing.

The Gamakatsu hooks do complement the fine lines that are now essential for use with the pole and I know that many other hook manufacturers are working on new and equally suitable patterns.

These will be evaluated and put into service as and when they arrive on the market, but at the moment the hooks we have mentioned, are to our minds, the best currently available for the various baits and venues.

Due to the very fine nature of the wire, great care must be taken when unhooking fish as Wayne has mentioned. I never use a metal hook disgorger these days. The new plastic ones are much kinder to the hooks and the whipping, and with practice unhooking can be done just as quickly when using a disgorger as it can be by hand. Always ensure you have a good number of the various sizes of disgorgers with you as spares. They only cost a few pence, but if you lose one and do not have a spare with you it can cost you pounds in winnings.

Although we still use barbless hooks on various occasions with the running line, it is seldom that we use them with the pole, especially when we need to unship the pole to land a fish. A barbed hook is essential for this type of fishing. I do still sometimes use them when long line fishing to hand on reasonably fast flowing waters and when the catch rate is very high, but when the bites are few and far between I use the lighter micro-barbed patterns.

When we use the fly hooks in Ireland the hooks are not attached to the line by the upturned eye, they are whipped on like a spade end. The purpose of the eye is to prevent the maggots being blown up the line. The barb is squeezed down slightly to aid penetration but is not completely flattened as this would allow the maggots to keep flying off. Under these conditions you must keep bait changes to a minimum, catching as many fish as possible between them. Often we are still catching steadily on just the skins.

No matter what size or type of hook you need to use, they must be changed at the slightest sign of the points breaking down. You can tell when you are baiting up whether the point has blunted at all. It may still look sharp, but if it will not snick easily through the skin of the bait without bursting it then it is faulty and requires changing. This is particularly important when pole fishing. Due to the cushioning effect of the elastic, hook penetration will be reduced if this happens, and you cannot afford to bump fish off in a match situation.

It is surprising how many match anglers particularly at club level, still buy hooks ready tied to nylon. Although some of the top patterns are now available ready tied, the only way of being certain that you have the correct pattern of hook balanced to the diameter and type of line you want, is to learn to tie your own. Otherwise you will never be able to take advantage of the range of tackle now available.

Please remember — litter loses fishing

Pole Elastic

Q. *What elastic system do you use and how do you balance your elastic strength to your hook size and hooklength with regard to the different species and waters?.*

Wayne: For me personally there is only one system that I use and that is the internal elastic system over the top two sections, or, just in the top section if it is long enough. It is out the way of the wind or other external factors and is virtually foolproof. It is under tension all of the time so cannot tangle or get caught up or damaged, and provided it is examined and changed regularly no problems should arise. This is where a lot of people slip up. They do not check for wear at the bung or where it is connected to the stonfo connector, and in the summer especially, it can start to perish at these points due to the wear and the heat. I always use the 'slip' lubricant. This helps to reduce the wear and allows the elastic to perform properly, at the same time keeping it in good condition. Just by virtue of pulling out the elastic to apply the lubricant, you can spot any signs of the elastic starting to break down and it is important to carry spare elastic in various strengths with you, plus an elastic threading wire, so that any necessary replacements can be made at the bankside. Spare stonfo connectors should also be carried just in case of a rare breakage.

The only other thing you need to look out for is where the elastic can rub on the inner wall of the pole when the pole is bending under the weight of a fish. This can sometimes cause wear on the elastic, although this is minimised by the use of the 'slip' lubricant. This is why some pole anglers prefer to have the elastic running externally through rings whipped onto the upper sections, but to my mind this makes it unnecessarily cumbersome and untidy and providing you check and change your elastic on a regular basis no problems should arise.

Balancing the grade of elastic to the size of fish you are expecting to catch is also very important, it is just as essential as balancing your line strength and hook size.

The elastic is graded by numbers 1 to 8, the larger the number, the

Table 1

Colour Code	Hook Size	Hook Length	Main Line
Red	26–22	8 oz–12 oz	1 lb–1 ¼ lb
Green	24–20	12 oz–1 lb	1 ¼ lb–1 ½ lb
Blue	22–18	1 lb–1 ½ lb	1 ½ lb–2 lb
Black	20–14	1 ½ lb–2 ½ lb	3 lb–3 ½ lb
White	18–14	2 lb–3 lb	3 lb–4 lb

thicker the elastic. Alongside this number coding is a colour coding; red, green, blue, black and white. Most anglers and tackle dealers work by the colour coding and to make explanation easier the reader should refer to the chart supplied in the text when working out the correct balance of line strength and hook size.

For general fishing I use the green coded elastic in conjunction with the recommended hook sizes and line strengths. For river fishing where I think I may tangle with a few chub I will step up to the blue elastic. For canal work where the fish are expected to be on the small side I would use the red elastic, but if I thought a few decent fish in the 4 or 5 oz range were likely I would go for the green elastic. As you will see from the chart, many of the hook and line sizes overlap each other, so the size of fish you are expecting to catch is the final deciding factor in the choice of elastic.

The bigger the fish, the stronger the elastic. If you try to swing a 5 or 6 oz fish in on too fine an elastic, that's when it starts to bounce and you risk the hook coming out. Slightly stronger elastic also helps with the hook penetration which is also an important consideration where larger fish are concerned. If you have a run of losing fish off the hook you need to decide whether this is due to the elastic being too soft and not allowing you to drive the hook home, or the elastic being too strong, causing the hook to pull out. This really is a catch 22 situation. If this should happen I would normally, where possible, go for the stronger elastic and better penetration, increasing the hook size if I thought I could get away with it.

When we come to the heavier black or white elastics, we are looking at situations where large fish such as carp, tench or chub are the target species. Under these circumstances forged hooks as opposed to fine wire hooks would normally be used. Forged hooks such as the Kamatsu B920 are very strong, but still relatively fine in the wire when compared to traditional flattened bronze hooks. The Gamakatsu 6325 series are also worth considering under these circumstances.

Don: It is very important not to cut your pole tip back too far when

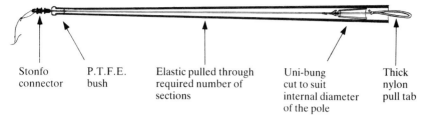

| Stonfo
connector | P.T.F.E.
bush | Elastic pulled through
required number of
sections | Uni-bung
cut to suit
internal diameter
of the pole | Thick
nylon
pull tab |

Fig. 1. Sectional view of internal elastic system

fitting your P.T.F.E. bush. In the early days when only one or two sizes of bush were available, the tendency was to cut back the pole to suit the size of the bush. These days a larger range of bush sizes is available and this is unnecessary. If possible, with the red or green elastic, we prefer to only have this in the very top section, as it stretches very easily and it is unnecessary to have it over two sections. On flowing water, the extra pole action achieved by having a longer tip helps you to 'feel' the fish and play it properly, with less chance of bumping it off.

When using the heavier elastics such as the blue, black and white, then we do put this through two or more top sections as we will be expecting to catch larger fish.

Many poles now are available with an option of spare top sections. This allows you to have a long flexible top for use with finer elastic for general fishing, with a shorter, stiffer tip for the stronger elastic for the bigger fish. Many anglers now use the pole for carp fishing on lakes and providing you are geared up properly for them it's surprising just what size of fish you can get out. Obviously, if you hook something 10 lb plus it's in the lap of the gods if you get it out or not, but for 2½ to 5 lb fish, it is amazing how quickly they can be played out on 1½ lb to 2 lb hooklengths. Again it all comes down to balancing your tackle to suit the fish you are after. Providing you have a full understanding of how it all works, the pole will do the job for you.

Just to re-cap on the basics: the elastic is fitted between the first or first and second sections of the pole and connected at the lower end to a conical bung, cut to suit your pole's diameter at that point. (see fig. 1). These are available from all good dealers. The elastic at the tip is connected to a stonfo connector, onto which you loop your tackle, locking it in position with the attached sleeve. The stonfo connector has a sleeve on each end. One slides over your elastic which is tied onto it with a simple half hitch knot, and the other slides over the hook onto which you loop your tackle. Once the elastic has been tensioned this then butts up to the end of your P.T.F.E. bush, which is slid either externally onto the pole tip or internally into the hollow of the tip. (see fig. 2).

Wire elastic threaders are also available from tackle shops and are a worthwhile investment. It is virtually impossible to thread your elastic through the pole without one.

Flyline or backing cord is tied to the end of the bung to allow you to pull it out when you need to change your elastic. Thick monofilament can also be used for this job. It runs down the middle of the joint when the next section is fitted on. If your pole is of the 'put over' type you must ensure that the bung is far enough up the pole to allow you to fit in the next section joint.

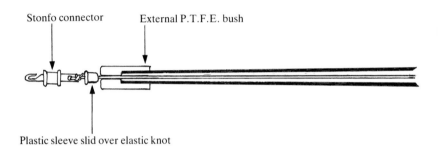

Stonfo connector   External P.T.F.E. bush

Plastic sleeve slid over elastic knot

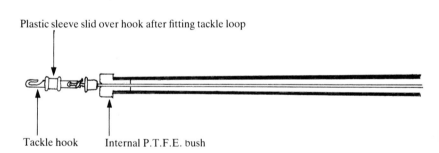

Plastic sleeve slid over hook after fitting tackle loop

Tackle hook   Internal P.T.F.E. bush

Fig. 2. External and internal P.T.F.E. bushes

1989/1990 Shakespeare Superteam

Left to right—back row: Tony Lockett—Product Engineer, Stuart Hartford, Dave Harrell, Steve Pierpoint, Stan Peicha, Kim Milsom, Frank Barlow, Tony Davis, John Tomsett—Managing Director

Seated: Don Slaymaker, Steve Webb, Ken Giles, Tony Eaves, Maurice Dutfield, Wayne Swinscoe.

Don about to net a Long Higgin bream during an evening match on the Trent.

Wayne's selection of stillwater pole floats. These few tackles cover most of his stillwater
pole-fishing requirements.

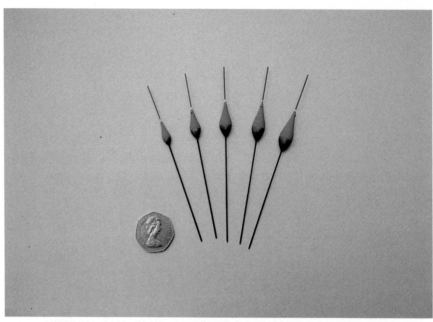

These cane-stemmed 'Team England' floats are ideal for stillwater pole fishing.

Super-slim, cane-stemmed floats for squatt and pinkie fishing on canals.

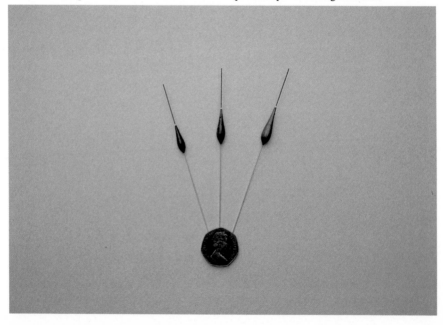

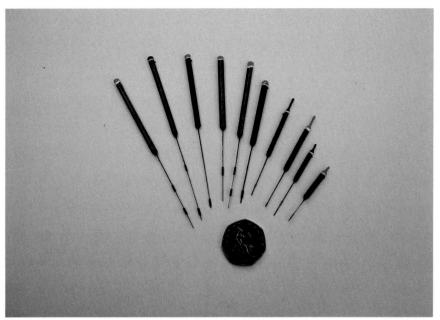

A selection of homemade wire-stem peacock 'Dibbers', essential for caster fishing on canals.

Popular float patterns for use on slow-moving rivers and drains.

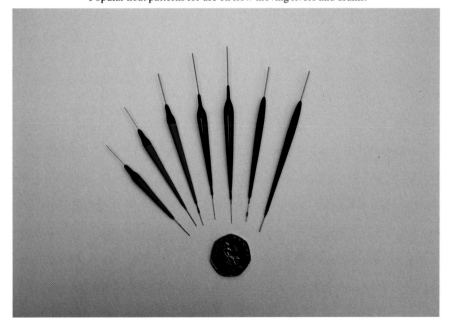

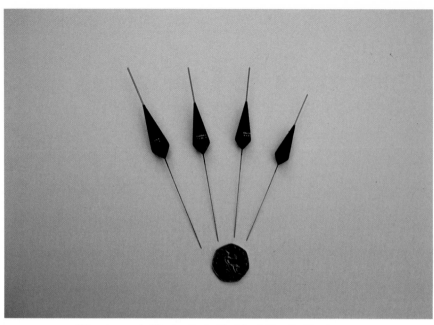

Wire-stemmed stillwater floats, ideal for fishing the bloodworm.

Another popular pole fishing float pattern.

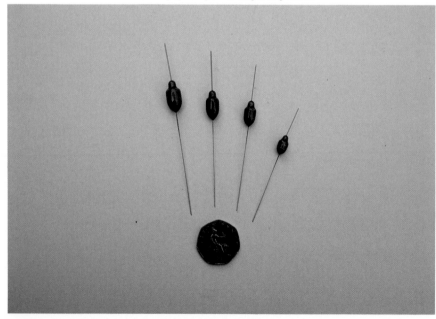

Fresh bloodworm, the most effective 'natural' bait.

Squatts, an effective alternative canal bait when bloodworm is barred.

Shakespeare Superteam member Kim Milsom feeds back the pole in readiness to unship and land a bream at Holme Pierrepont Rowing Course. Note the cooler box in the foreground for transporting his fragile jokers and bloodworms.

With the pole now unshipped, Kim prepares to land the fish. Note the full length of pole is at hand to be put back on quickly if the fish makes a last desperate run.

Pole Floats

Q. *Over the years, hundreds of float patterns have come and gone for use with the running line and for practical purposes these have been reduced to variations of just a few basic types. The same thing is happening again with pole floats. Dozens of different patterns using different shapes and material combinations are flooding the market, all claiming superiority for certain specific situations. Can you please put this into perspective and tell us which basic float patterns you use in most of the situations covering still waters, canals and rivers?.*

Wayne: On flowing rivers, regardless of the pace, be it fast or slow, you need a float with a shoulder at the top of the body. This can be a completely round body or a reversed pear shape, but to make it work properly on those occasions, when you need to hold back and slow the tackle down, it must have this shoulder for the water to hold it down beneath the surface (see figs. 16–17). I use these basic types of float for 99% of my pole fishing on rivers. One of the biggest problems with these types of float is that the wire or cane stems are too short. This makes them less stable than I like them to be, and I often pull out the stems and fit them with longer ones. If the float manufacturers would increase the stem length by 75 to 100% they would work a lot better. Some of the new imported floats are now coming onto the market with these extra long stems and hopefully these will overcome the problem, but they are very expensive when compared to English made floats. On very slow flowing drains where I expect to get a lot of drop bites, I sometimes use a thinner, longer bodied float similar to the shape of a stick float with a bristle in the tip, used in conjunction with spaced out shotting or styl leads. For still-water fishing I use floats with the same pear shaped body, but with the thin end uppermost. In other words, the reverse of the river floats (see fig. 4). I carry a full range of these from .25 grammes upwards, and these cover all of my still-water and canal fishing require-ments except for when caster fishing over on the far ledge of the narrower canals. Then I use what we call a peacock 'dibber', which, as the name implies is just a short, thin piece of peacock quill with a fine wire stem

Elastic being pulled out of pole tip. Note the P.T.F.E. bush on the end of the pole and the 'stonfo' connector on the end of the elastic

without a bristle in the tip. This is normally fished connected to the bottom end only and dotted down so only a tiny dimple is showing on the surface. (see fig. 11).

These are the three basic types of floats that we use for the majority of our pole fishing, and you can judge by our results as to whether we are doing it right or not.

The variety of pole floats now available on the market is mind blowing, even to those of us who fish regularly, so what it's like for the lads who are just getting into it I do not know, it must be terribly confusing. I have got boxes full of pole floats that I have bought on impulse, or people have given to me, but I never use them. For some reason they do not look right or feel right and as I have great confidence in the patterns I have described, I have no call to use them. The ones I am currently using are beginning to look a bit battered and tatty now, but when I do replace them it will be with floats of a similar type.

Don: It seems to me that the float manufacturers are having a contest between themselves as to who can bring out the most different shapes. It may be good for business but it does not help the angler very much. Most of them are just variations of the same basic theme, so why bother buying them all when the basic patterns we have described will do the same job?

As Wayne has already said, there is room for improvement with commercial floats, but this has more to do with the stem length than with the body shape. If they could be made with the stems 1½″ to 2″ longer the floats would be a lot more stable, particularly in windy conditions. We use extra long stick floats and wagglers in these conditions, so why not pole floats? The same basic principles still apply to them as well. The big problem is getting hold of the right gauge of wire or size of cane with which to make or modify the floats to suit.

Wayne: Yes, this is a problem, fortunately we have a good float manufacturer in Nottingham and we can always go round and pinch a bit off of him!.

Don: Some of us can!. I don't seem to have enough cheek to do it. But we have been working on the problem and hopefully it will not be too long before the types of floats we need will come onto the market.

The type of stem material is also very important. When short lining the wire stems are ideal, but for long lining on the rivers we find the thin cane stems preferable. I think the reason for this is that because the cane stem floats are lighter, they follow the olivette or shots out on the cast better, without having that inter-action between the weight and the float that you often get with the heavier stem floats. It does make a lot of difference to your accuracy, particularly in windy conditions.

The exception to this is when bloodworm fishing where a nice long fine wire stem seems to perform the best.

The only other problem is in the thickness of the bristle. Whilst a nice fine bristle is visible in calm conditions, it is very difficult to see them on exposed waters in windy, choppy conditions. For river fishing when long lining, a much thicker bristle is needed when fishing at 7 or 8 metres out. One dodge when visibility is a problem, is to slide a long piece of thin brightly coloured, or in some cases black, silicon tubing over the existing bristle to increase the thickness and the visibility. Unfortunately, very few manufacturers have seen the necessity of bringing out floats of the same sizes and patterns with different thicknesses of bristle. They still work on the principle of the bigger the float the thicker the bristle, not realising that you often need to have a thicker bristle on a smaller float. Different anglers also have different degrees of eyesight and those with sight problems are often put off pole fishing because of this.

Other Equipment

Q. *What part does the fashionable trend of using platform and continental style tackle carriers play in your approach to pole fishing?.*

Wayne: These are very expensive pieces of equipment so personally, I weigh up the benefits of them carefully and I am only prepared to justify the expense if they give me a positive advantage. With regard to platforms—I feel that these are an essential investment for any angler who is going to use a pole on a regular basis. When you are using a pole, especially a long pole, you must be comfortable and stable and have everything to hand. Often, especially when river fishing on rocks, rough banks, or in shallow margins this is not always possible, even with adjustable legs on your tackle box. Often you can get your box fairly stable but you are unable to get your other equipment laid out. Or, when fishing in shallow margins, your seat box clear of the water.

When you are fishing with a rod and reel, you can fish any peg standing up or sitting down at will, as you have no weight to cope with. You can bend down for your maggots or groundbait quite easily without any problems.

With 11 metres of pole stuck out you cannot manipulate yourself very well to go down and pick up bait etc. Your pole splashes on the water and it is very difficult to get into an efficient rhythm.

The introduction of the platforms that we have seen over the last few years are a very good idea. Obviously it takes a bit more effort transporting your gear to the peg and a little more time setting it all up, but you do get yourself very comfortable. Once you are set up everything is to hand and this helps you to fish efficiently and smoothly. As for the very expensive continental tackle carriers that are now very popular, personally I am not really in favour of these. They are very heavy and if you fish a lot of different venues which often involve long walks over very rough terrain, and difficult pegs where you cannot always get everything down to the waters edge, they can be a handicap.

I find the standard plastic seat boxes far more versatile. They are lighter and more durable and I have never found any difficulty in getting

Wayne's orderly tackle layout, essential for efficiency and speed. Note the platform in this instance is used for tackle and bait. Wayne uses a purpose built pole fishing stool with adjustable legs and built in pole rests. Under the seat cushion is a tackle compartment.

all of my equipment into them. By using the specially designed tackle boxes with removable trays that fit into the top of the box, I have more than enough room for all of the other equipment such as reels, catapults, bait trays and pole tackle boxes etc.

Don: I think that the latest platforms and the continental boxes are brilliant. They are quite expensive but if you can afford them I personally feel that they are a worthwhile investment. If an angler has a limited budget then the priority must be the purchase of a platform. These are an essential, whereas the tackle boxes are a luxury as opposed to a necessity. As Wayne has said, you have got to be comfortable when pole fishing and a platform does give you this comfort.

The other important consideration is height. This is very difficult to explain, as only each individual can assess which is the right height to be at above the water to fish effectively. But it is essential to have your back straight and to hold the pole at the correct angle and when short line fishing, for the pole tip to be at the correct height above the float. The adjustable legs on the platform allow you to control this.

Often we fish with the platform at the side of our seat box, using it as a bait and tackle stand. On other occasions we will have the platform actually in the water with our seat box on the top of it just clear of the surface. A fantastic range of attachments for pole rests, keep net mountings, bait trays etc are now available to fit the platforms, ensuring that no matter what type of bank you need to fish off, you can get everything laid out for maximum efficiency. The bolt-on adjustable legs are also a very recent but effective innovation and when used in conjunction with a platform can give you even greater control over your height, particularly when you need to stand them in the shallow margins of the river or lake.

Manufacturers are now putting a lot more thought into the design of auxiliary equipment to help the match angler fish more effectively, and anyone cosidering taking up match fishing at open level must be prepared to invest in the most efficient equipment available to be able to compete properly.

Baits

Q. *What baits do you use when pole fishing and what is involved in their preparation and keeping them in good condition?*

Wayne: At the moment I think I can honestly say that 90% of our fishing is centred around the use of maggot baits in their various forms i.e. maggots, squatts, pinkies and casters. This applies to both still as well as flowing waters. If we are going to a specialised venue then we do take bloodworm and jokers, you have to if you are to compete, but these occasions are few and far between and are mainly restricted to winter team events on canals.

Early on in the season, if it's a long hot summer, the caster still takes some beating on those venues that respond to it, such as Long Higgin on the River Trent. On this water, which is now an out and out pole venue, we feed caster and ground bait and use red maggot on the hook. Small and large skimmers have taken over from the roach as the target species during the summer months and bream of any sort do tend to prefer red maggots. Having said that, I feel that this preference for red maggots is a trend that anglers have brought to the bream as opposed to the other way around, but the important thing is that currently this is what they like, so this is what you must use.

On roach venues the bronze maggot, where allowed, is still the most effective bait, and I always clean mine off really well, adding a little Tumeric powder to them the night before the match and again at the bankside.

Squatts and pinkies are also an essential bait particularly on still-waters and canals and these can be used as feeders and as hookbaits, or as feeders with bronze or red maggots on the hook.

Don: Yes I have to agree, I would never go to a roach venue without an adequate supply of bronze maggots, currently they are the best bait. Even with the increased cost of maggots you must take a sufficient quantity of good, clean, fresh bait with you to a match if you intend to compete effectively. The worst thing in the world that could happen is to draw on a big shoal of hungry fish and then run out of bait halfway through the match. During the summer months a minimum of six to eight pints of maggots is needed on rivers such as the Trent or the Warwickshire Avon, which contain large heads of fish. Although this book is primarily concerned with pole fishing and we do now use a pole far more than ever before on these venues, this method is also used in conjunction with the running line, so we still need to feed two or even three lines of the river on a continual basis throughout the match. This cannot be done effectively with just a couple of pints of bait. Preparation is very important, just as important as the quality of the bait.

I usually collect my bait from the tackle shop the day before the match and riddle it off, removing all the old meal or sawdust and any dead maggots or skins. I then put it into a large container to prevent sweating and add fresh maize meal. After a couple of hours I sieve the bait again, removing the meal and add fresh meal and Tumeric. The bait is then put in the fridge overnight. If I have chance I will sieve it again on the morning of the match, adding fresh meal and Tumeric. This ensures that the bait is really clean and free from grease. The Tumeric as well as adding flavour also helps to remove the grease, allowing the bait to sink quickly. This is essential when pole fishing on a river.

With regard to preparing casters; we are fortunate in this area to have access to top quality commercially produced casters from our local dealers, and we do not have the time to produce our own. Even if we did have the time, it still would not pay economically to bother with turning our own anyway. It takes 8 pints of maggots to produce 4 or 5 pints of casters, so you waste 3 pints. Providing the quality of shop-bought casters is good then it is cheaper in terms of both time and money to buy them in.

It is important that the casters you get are fresh and as soon as you get home you need to wash them and remove any maggots or dead skins. At this stage I normally put a handful in an open container in the fridge, to turn into floaters for use on the hook, and the rest are put into a bait container so that it is filled to within ¼″ from the top. Then I put cling film over the top before fitting on the lid and keep them overnight in the fridge. This is far more preferable than leaving them in a plastic bag as it prevents 'bag burn' where the casters touch the plastic. When opened for use the casters kept in the bait container will be as fresh as when you put them in, and once at the waterside you can cover them with water to prevent them turning into floaters during the course of the match.

Pinkies are usually riddled off and put into fresh sawdust. This is preferable to maize meal as it is more absorbent. Pinkies will climb at any hint of dampness, so this quality is very important. Squatts can be riddled off and any dead skins removed. They are then normally returned to the sand you buy them in, ensuring it is damp enough to keep them in good condition. The container can then be kept in the 'warmest' part of the fridge which is usually at the bottom. Squatts are very fragile and cannot stand direct sunlight. Always keep them in the shade under your umbrella on hot sunny days, continually dampening the sand to prevent it drying out. Most match anglers take a fine mesh squatt riddle with them to a match, riddling off the squatts a few at a time as and when they are required. Many of them transport squatts and bloodworm and jokers to the match in portable cooling boxes such as those used by picnickers, ensuring that they arrive in good condition. We will discuss the preparation and keeping of bloodworm and jokers more fully in the chapter on bloodworm fishing.

Q. *You mentioned the use of groundbait in conjunction with casters when fishing for skimmers. How much of a part does groundbaiting play in your approach to pole fishing, and what type of mixes do you use with regard to various baits and species?.*

Wayne: Early on in the season, on venues which respond to its use, we do use quite a lot of groundbait. If anything, groundbait is currently neglected, but with the increased cost of maggots I can see it playing a much greater role in the future. With regard to the mixes we use, I am increasingly using more and more of the continental mixes in conjunction with standard brown crumb. The various types of continental brands do allow for a greater variation in the way the bait can be made to work and it is this physical property that attracts me to it rather than the smell of it. Different brands do have different properties with regard to their binding qualities, so I do use different types for different waters.

For most of my fishing on the Trent when I am going to use ground-bait, which I normally use in conjunction with caster and hemp during the summer months for skimmers, I will mix between 50% and 75% of standard fine brown crumb with a binder depending upon how heavy I want to make it. Obviously when pole fishing I will want it to go down quickly and not be taken down the swim out of pole range. The depth and rate of flow will be taken into consideration when blending the mix, and the type of binder used and the ratio of brown crumb will be adjusted accordingly. For a really heavy mix I will use Van den Eynde Secret, and for a lighter mix I will use Beet. I always try to use as much brown crumb as possible for economic reasons, as it is far cheaper. But if the nature of the swim dictates a lesser proportion of brown crumb then I have to balance the mix to suit the conditions. The important consideration is of course to get the feed down to where you want it and for it to break up how you want it too. There are no hard and fast rules. You can only learn the correct balance of ingredients by experience.

Don: I use more or less the same mix as Wayne but I also like to use the ground hemp in with the mix as well. Although it is quite expensive, I do feel that it is a very good attractor and I really have confidence in it, which is a very important consideration. It is possible to use white groundbait as a binder, but I prefer to keep my groundbait a darker colour and the products Wayne has mentioned suit me for this reason. If the added ingredients do, as they claim, attract and stimulate a feeding response then fair enough, that is an added bonus, but as Wayne has mentioned it is how they help to bind the mix and control its breakup that is the important consideration.

It is important to use the right loose feed mixed in with the ground bait; casters, squatts and hemp are the normal types and on occasions pinkies when a quicker breakup is needed. Big maggots are not normally used as they cause the balls to break up either in mid air or too high up in the water.

Strangely enough when using casters in the groundbait, it is seldom that it works with using caster on the hook as well. We nearly always use a big red or bronze maggot as our hookbait. The number of times I have tried using caster on the hook and have been unable to get a bite is countless, yet as soon as I change to a maggot on the hook I am getting a bite every swim down. This method is particularly effective on the deeper slower stretches of the Trent such as you find at Long Higgin or Radcliffe Viaduct.

If we feel that a better stamp of fish could be caught with caster on the hook, then we have found that it is better to loose feed the casters in conjunction with loose fed hemp and leave the groundbait alone.

Wayne: With regard to fishing still waters with smaller baits such as squatts or pinkies, then we would use a different sort of mix altogether. For this type of fishing we will use Van den Eynde Supercup in conjunction with brown crumb. This fluffs up nicely and can be mixed to break up on impact with the water, forming a slowly sinking cloud of groundbait and squatts, attracting fish such as roach and skimmers on the drop. Again it is the physical properties of the brand which we are considering, as opposed to its smell. My opinion is that although you can smell it on the bank, as soon as it hits the water in the middle of a lake, any scent is going to dissolve in seconds and become non-effective. On a flowing water where it is going down in the same spot every time then it could have some effect, but I would not set too much store by it. As Don has said, if it does have an effect then that is a bonus, but I have tried most of the various additives that have come onto the market and to me they have made no difference. On hard days the fish have not switched on when I have used them, and when they have been feeding they take the bait anyway, regardless of whether I have used an additive or not. The important thing is bait quality and presentation. This is the real key to success.

Pole Fishing on Still Waters

Q. *Because of the differences between pole fishing approaches on different types of waters, I want to cover each type separately, including its own specific tackle, shotting, tactics and feeding methods.*

Let us first discuss your approach to still waters and slow moving rivers and drains. How do you go about assessing your swim and deciding upon your basic approach?

Don: The important consideration is the current form of the venue you are going to fish and the species you can expect to catch. This will not only influence the nature of your tackle but also what baits you are going to take.

On venues that we fish regularly we know by experience what the form is at various points in the season, and we very seldom get it wrong. The real problems arise on unknown or distant venues that we need to fish on summer knockout competitions with the Superteam. Then we really do have to do our homework by ringing around match anglers who we know fish these venues regularly or by visiting the venues ourselves on practice sessions and try to put it together from there.

Whatever the venue there are basic rules that do apply and once these are fully understood then in most circumstances they can be applied to any still water situations.

Under the new N.F.A. match rules you are now allowed to plumb your depth and test the shotting of your tackle prior to the start of the match and it is important to take advantage of this. On any still water, be it a pond, lake, river or drain, as we include sluice controlled rivers, such as the north bank of the Nene, the Huntspill, the Welland and the Witham etc as still waters, you always try to locate features such as shelves and ledges, sand and gravel bars, hollows or depressions in lake beds, weed beds, anything that may be considered as a fish holding or feeding areas, and you will always feed and fish to these. So five or ten minutes spent searching out these features and establishing the overall geography of your swim is very important.

The next main consideration which will dictate the type of rigs that you will use is the species of fish that you are likely to catch, or need to catch if you are to stand a chance of winning the match.

Many still waters are mixed species waters, so if it is an individual event you must go for the match winning species. If these are bream or skimmers then bottom fishing tactics will be used, groundbaiting with squatts and casters or if bloodworm is allowed, jokers. If the target species are roach, then loose feeding tactics are generally employed, fishing strung out Styl leads for fishing on the drop, or in colder conditions when the fish are feeding on or near the bottom, an olivette rig.

On waters that have a series of features at different ranges, then a couple of lines will be fed to help to maintain a steady catch rate, alternating between them as and when you feel that one of them should be rested. Often, it takes a while before the bream move in, so if there are roach present these can be caught steadily on a closer line until such time as the bream line starts to produce.

On some waters that are fairly uniform in depth and relatively featureless, you then normally fish out at a comfortable distance with regards to the wind conditions and feed the fish into the swim.

Wayne: The beauty of pole fishing is that you can, by virtue of the pole tip being directly over the tackle, plumb the depth very accurately. I normally start off by setting the float to the depth at maximum range and then gradually work back towards me. As the peg starts to shallow off this will be shown by the float being increasingly above the surface of the water. Any holes or depressions will be indicated by the float sinking below the surface. It is important to have a relatively heavy plummet to allow you to achieve the correct 'feel' (see fig 3). As we have already mentioned in the chapter on floats, the usual pattern that we use on still waters is the pear-shaped type with the narrow part of the body towards the top. These can be fished with either an olivette when bottom fishing or with strung out shots or Styl leads for fishing 'on the drop'. In many ways the Styl leads, whilst admittedly more fiddly to put on, are superior to split shots when weights need to be shuffled around during the course of a match to vary the presentation. They have finely machined centres which fit 'around' the line as opposed to a 'vee' which tightens 'on' the line. This minimises the risks of line damage whilst they are being moved about.

These days, most of my floats for use with general baits such as maggot and caster on still waters have cane stems. They seem far less prone to tangles with the terminal tackle, but I still prefer wire stemmed floats for bloodworm fishing. I do not know why but for some reason I hit far more bites with these.

A basic bottom fishing rig is shown in fig. 7. On still waters the

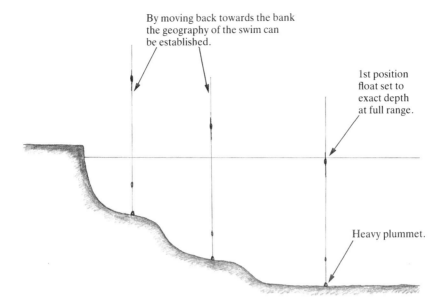

By moving back towards the bank the geography of the swim can be established.

1st position float set to exact depth at full range.

Heavy plummet.

Fig. 3. Plumbing the depth

olivette is positioned 6 in to 12 in from the hook, with one or two small droppers, depending upon the length of tail. The bait is positioned just off or just on the bottom depending upon how the fish are feeding, but for bloodworm the bait is usually fished just off the bottom. As you can see, very accurate plumbing of the depth is essential.

The size of olivette is determined by a number of factors; the depth of the water, the strength of the wind or undertow and the distance at which you are fishing.

Although in reasonable conditions you can fish with a small, light float and olivette at a distance, visibility of the bristle is often a problem and a larger float and olivette often needs to be used to allow you to fish with a thicker bristle. Obviously in windy conditions, heavier floats and olivettes are needed to keep the rig stable. Bigger floats with larger bodies and longer stems are an advantage in these circumstances.

Q. *What signs would you look for during the course of the match and what changes would you make to your tackle and feeding in response?*

Don: When fishing on the drop, the same principles of moving shots

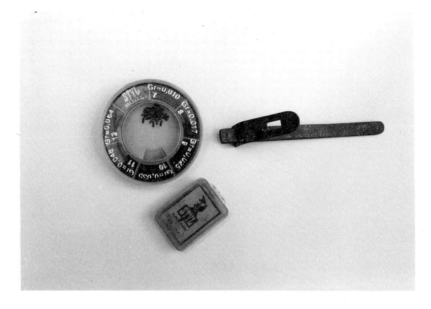

Styl leads and pincers for crimping them on the line

or Styl leads about to vary the presentation still applies to pole fishing as it does with the running line.

Normally we start off with the weights strung out evenly at full depth, as shown in fig. 4. If the fish then start to come up in the water we will shallow off and lighten off by moving some of the leads directly under the float (see fig. 5).

If the fish stay near the bottom we will move the weights down to below half depth to give us a faster sink and get down to the fish more quickly (see fig. 6). Some times we may just change poles, as often when fishing still waters we will have two poles set up, one with a bottom fishing rig and one with a drop rig. This allows us to alternate between the two styles as and when the conditions dictate.

Many anglers find it useful to mark the original depth on their poles with an elastic band or typewriter correction fluid so that they can return it quickly after shallowing off without having to re-plumb. This can be a real time saver if you need to alter your depth a number of times during a session.

Often, in the summer months, when most of our still water fishing takes place, the fish do tend to move about a lot at all levels in the water, particularly small skimmers and roach, so the versatility of the Styl rig for this type of fishing really comes into its own. When this happens,

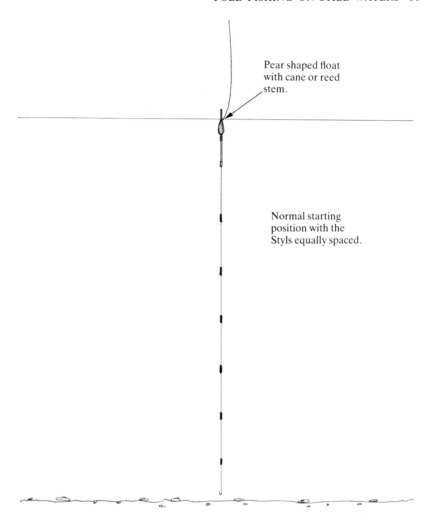

Pear shaped float
with cane or reed
stem.

Normal starting
position with the
Styls equally spaced.

Fig. 4. Basic stillwater Styl rig

bites are indicated by a delay in the settling of the float as well as by
the float going under, so it is important to note the timing in the fall
of the leads or shot so that any delay can be identified.

The feed rate needs to be very carefully measured to keep the fish
coming. It is important to keep putting in sufficient feed to hold the
interest of the fish but not too much so as to over feed them or have

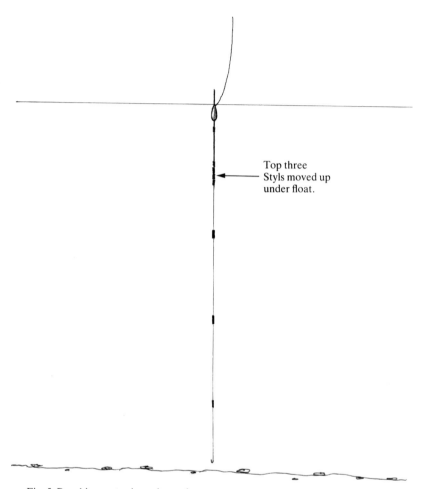

Top three Styls moved up under float.

Fig. 5. Bunching up to give a slower drop

the fish moving back down towards the bottom by chasing surplus feed that may fall past them. By introducing the correct amount at regular intervals the fish will be competing with each other for the bait, making for positive bites on a regular basis. At the slightest sign of any fall of the bite rate, the feed needs to be cut back proportionally. If the bite rate increases then the feed can be increased to suit. Always measure your feeding to the response of the fish. This is especially important on still waters, as unlike river fishing, the surplus feed will not get washed away, but will pile up on the bottom, reducing the chances of your hook bait being taken.

Wayne: Yes, this point is very important. Many anglers feed out of habit rather than with consideration to the response of the fish. Having said that, with regard to what Don has said about mid water feeding fish following surplus feed down to the bottom, I have a different theory about this and I must mention it even though it will probably confuse the issue rather than clarify it, but that I am afraid is the nature of angling.

When you get a lot of fish feeding on the drop they will often ignore bait that is going past them, feeding only on that which they can see coming down to them, particularly in warm weather. On these days they are only feeding in the top half of the water and unless you keep the bait going in they will just drift off somewhere else. You may only get odd bites to start with but the activity will attract other fish into the area and then things will get really hectic.

When they are pre-occupied with feeding like this they will be constantly looking upwards for their food.

On the Welland and Nene and similar Fenland waters this can often be a deadly method. You will only get odd bites for a start, but then when you probably have not had a bite for half an hour or so, you will cast in and as you reach for your catapult your float will lift out of the water like a lighthouse and you connect with a big roach. This is a sign to start feeding more heavily. You might have ten chucks in after that and your tackle will sink to the bottom without getting a bite, then on the eleventh chuck in it will go again on the drop. As the day goes on you will get bites more and more frequently and you end up by fishing only a couple of feet deep, piling in the maggots and catching quality fish almost every cast in. The anglers around you will be standing watching motionless floats, hardly feeding anything in at all and wondering what the hell is going on.

This happened to me on several occasions last year and it was unbelievable. Both Don and I have had a lot of success on the north bank of the Nene in recent seasons using this method. Obviously there are areas where you want to draw and areas where you do not want to draw, but when we have been lucky enough to draw in those 20 or 30 pegs, even though we may not have been on the best of those pegs but are in the area where a lot of roach have been caught, then we have always done well.

Everyone starts off by fishing at full depth in 14 ft of water, but by the end of the match we have finished up by fishing only two feet deep whilst the rest of the field are still fishing on the bottom.

On other days then it will be as Don has said. They will often start by feeding on the bottom, rising up in the water in response to the loose

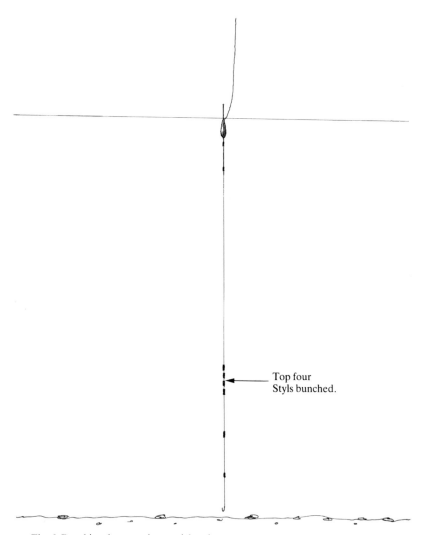

Top four
Styls bunched.

Fig. 6. Bunching down to give a quicker drop

feed, then after a while they will turn around and go back down again. Then you need to be careful just how much is going past them. You just need to gauge what sort of a day it is likely to be and unfortunately you can only do this by experience. The important thing is to be able to recognise what is happening and keep ringing the changes.

Wayne demonstrating the technique of supporting the pole with his right forearm whilst feeding with a catapult

Many anglers fail to make these important changes to their tackle and depth once the bites slow down, so they never identify when these situations occur. Because of this they do miss out on an awful lot of fish.

We have mentioned the use of groundbait with regard to bream fishing, but often a light cloud mix will also work well for catching roach and skimmers on the drop. Again, only practice and experience can tell you when and where to use it, but if you are catching steadily by using loose feeding tactics then it is pointless risking killing the swim by introducing groundbait, unless you are certain that the fish will respond.

When bream fishing a slightly heavier mix will be needed so that it breaks up on or near the bottom, as this will be where you will be concentrating your efforts. On mixed fisheries you will want to get you bait through the small fish to the bigger fish below. If you know that the match is going to be won with bream then you will not want your bait or your groundbiat being intercepted by small midwater feeding fish. A larger than usual float and olivette may have to be used to get it quickly through these fish and down to the bottom. A stiffer groundbait mix may also have to be used so that the smaller fish are less likely to be attracted to it.

Stepped up pole fishing tactics using heavier lines and elastic are now very effective for the more powerful still water species such as tench and carp, and many lakes are now being stocked with small carp for the match angler. It is often amazing just how fast the action can be on these venues and very big weights are now being achieved by using these heavy pole tactics.

Maggots, worms, casters and on some waters, seedbaits are used in conjunction with forged hooks, 1½ lb to 2 lbs hooklengths and stiff poles with heavy black or white grade elastic, and it is incredible how quickly fish of 3 or 4 lbs in weight can be subdued on this sort of tackle. On some of these waters match anglers are getting through 6 to 8 pints of bait in a session, unheard of amounts on most stillwater venues.

Don: Most stillwater pole fishing is accomplished by using short line tactics with only 12 in to 36 in of line between pole tip and float tip. This allows you complete control of the tackle in most conditions and due to the direct nature of this method, hitting bites is just a formality, a gentle lifting of the pole is all that is needed to connect with the fish.

There are odd occasions, particularly in windy conditions, when, due to the pole waving about in the wind, a longer length of line is needed to prevent the tackle being jerked about by the pole tip, spoiling the presentation.

Often this longer line is used in conjunction with a split shot placed midway between the float and the pole tip. This helps to absorb the movement of the pole tip, preventing the jerking of the line from being transmitted to the tackle (see fig. 7).

In very windy conditions some anglers switch to using a small fine tipped waggler or balsa antenna float, fixed bottom end only to the line when wind drift causes the conventional pole floats to move with the drift, again spoiling presentation. Now that poles have got a lot thinner, it is possible to hang on to a reasonable length of pole in these more extreme conditions, but generally speaking once these sort of tactics need to be resorted to it is time to switch to the running line anyway.

When fishing a long pole with a short line it is important to have a pole roller strategically placed behind you to allow the pole to be rapidly pushed back to the point where you need to unship it. As well as speeding up this process it also prevents any risk of knocking the end of the pole against obstacles and damaging the joint (see fig. 8).

I do not want to get too involved with basic pole handling techniques as these are adequately covered in the many beginner's books on pole fishing, but speed and competence in unshipping a long pole is an essential ability that needs to be mastered when pole fishing in a match situation. If the bank behind you is reasonably flat then the roller is normally placed behind you. If the bank behind you is steep then the roller is usually

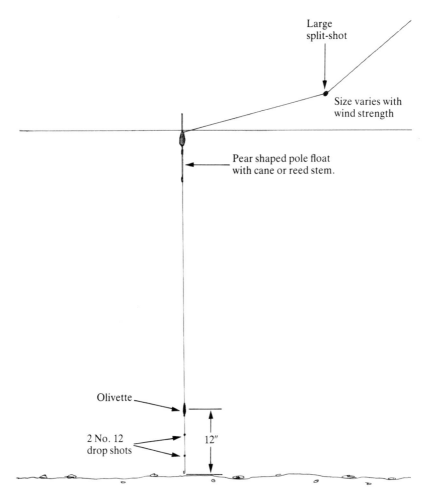

Large
split-shot

Size varies with
wind strength

Pear shaped pole float
with cane or reed stem.

Olivette

2 No. 12
drop shots

12"

Fig. 7. Basic stillwater olivette rig. Note addition of large shot between float and pole tip to prevent movement of the pole tip due to wind being transmitted to the float.

placed to one side and the pole is turned sideways whilst playing the fish and fed along the side of the bank. After a bit of practice this can be accomplished just as smoothly and quickly as can feeding the pole behind.

There are times when you may need to add sections rather than take them off. This is when carp or tench fishing. Carp will take your

Fig. 8. Using a pole roller to safely push back the pole to the un-shipping point

elastic out to the limit on their initial run and you often need to have a couple of extra sections at the side of you to quickly slip on to the pole so you can follow them out. The increased action that these extra sections allow will also help to cushion the force of this run once your elastic runs out of stretch. As the carp gradually becomes subdued you can begin to remove the sections one or two at a time, but you must be ready to slip them back on if the fish starts to run again. With smaller fish, the pole is fed back to the joint which allows you to swing the fish into your hand and the entire spare sections are unshipped in one complete length. If the fish requires netting you will unship a further section to give yourself enough line to allow the fish to be netted without lifting it out of the water.

Don't forget — discarded line kills birds and other wild animals

Pole Fishing on Canals

Q. *What rigs do you use for both close and long range pole fishing on canals and how do you vary them to cope with extreme conditions such as strong winds, surface skim and low water temperatures?*

Wayne: The pole has revolutionised canal fishing over the last few years and the advent of the long carbon poles has brought most aspects of canal fishing to within pole range. The only time the running line needs to be considered is on the big wide canals such as the Gloucester Canal, or on the larger Yorkshire canals such as the Stainforth and Keadby canal and the New Junction canal, which due to their width and exposed situation, light legering and waggler tactics often need to be employed in conjunction with pole tactics.

On the more traditional canal network the average width is only 12 to 14 metres or even less in some cases, and as most lengths tend to be tree lined on the more rural stretches they are relatively sheltered and wind problems are the exception rather than the rule.

The main baits to be considered are maggots, squatts, pinkies and casters, but where it is allowed, bloodworm and joker has now taken over as the supreme canal bait in many areas.

Whilst bloodworm and joker fishing will be mentioned where relevant in this chapter, its specific use will be covered in more detail in the chapter on bloodworm fishing.

Whilst we do not consider ourselves to be specialist canal anglers, we do, owing to our commitments with the Shakespeare Superteam find ourselves fishing an increasing number of canal venues in all areas of the country, so we can look at the methods employed in their broader context and hopefully be able to put them into perspective.

For maggot, squatt and pinkie fishing on the shallower canals with depths up to 3 to 4 ft, small versions of the cane stem pear-shaped stillwater floats will normally be employed with strung out micro-shot or Styl leads. For use with bloodworm we would use the same body pattern but with a wire stem, (see fig. 9) and this would be used in conjunction with an olivette or a piece of tungsten tubing when gudgeon fishing. For caster

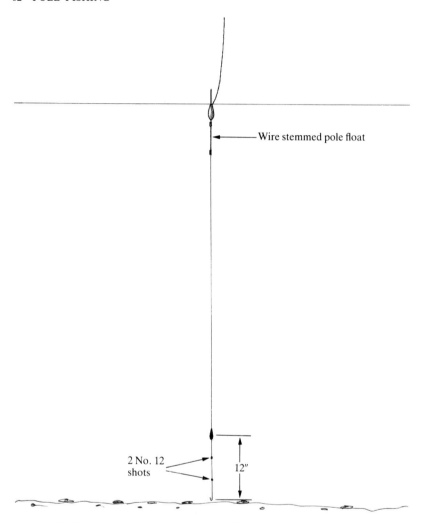

Fig. 9. Basic bottom fishing rig for bloodworm fishing on canals and stillwaters

fishing we use a completely different pattern. These are known as peacock 'dibbers'. They are made from a thin length of peacock with a fine wire stem that has a small eye near the top for fishing down the track (see fig. 10), or a shorter length with a shorter heavier gauge of wire stem, connected by the bottom end only for fishing right across on the top of the far ledge (see fig. 11). In both cases the floats are fished without

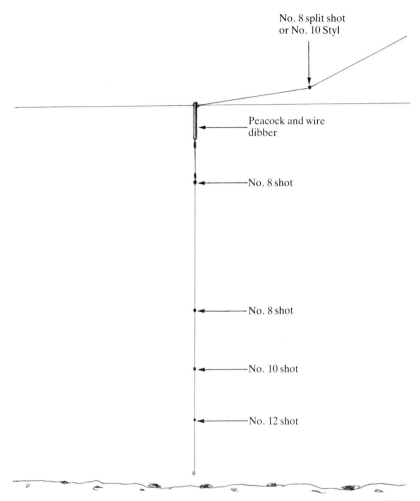

No. 8 split shot
or No. 10 Styl

Peacock and wire
dibber

No. 8 shot

No. 8 shot

No. 10 shot

No. 12 shot

Fig. 10. Dibber rig, for caster fishing on canals, can be fished across on the shelf
or down the track

a top bristle and are dotted right down so that the tip is almost flush
with the surface of the water.

In the case of the short far bank dibber, these are normally fished
on a longer line so that the pole tip is well to one side of the float as
opposed to the normal position of being directly over it. This is to prevent
the risk of the fish being spooked by the tip of the pole as the water
often tends to be clear and shallow on the top ledges of most of the

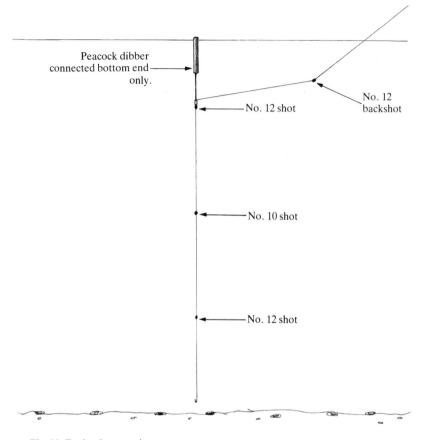

Fig. 11. Far bank caster rig

canals. Note the small back shot above the float, this helps to keep the line below the surface skim and prevents the rig from being pulled out of position.

Don: These caster rigs may seem very basic but they are also very effective. They are incredibly light and offer no resistance to a taking fish. Bites are generally positive and unmissable. Despite being popular with dedicated canal anglers, they are not readily available in commercial patterns with the degree of fineness that we consider essential, so most of us have to make our own. To ensure that the float only takes the amount of shot we want, one good tip is to make the float with a slightly longer

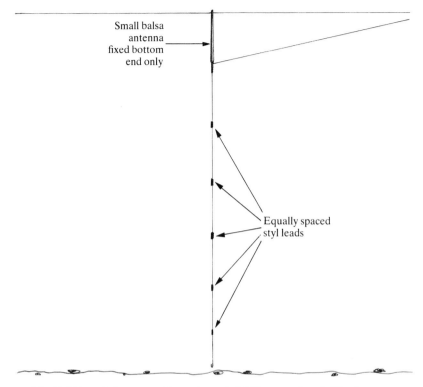

Small balsa
antenna
fixed bottom
end only

Equally spaced
styl leads

Fig. 12. Using a balsa antenna float to beat wind drift on canals and stillwaters

length of quill than you need, then after shotting it up and testing it
in a jug of water, mark and trim it to the correct length. The wires can
either be pinched from un-used commercial patterns for the finer ones
or for the thicker wires, the finest gauge of piano wire, which can be
bought from model shops can be used. The fine tip rings for the line
to go through can be made by winding a strand of 5 amp fuse wire
once around a pin or needle and twisting the ends together. A hole is
then poked into the side of the quill with a pin and the eye glued in.
    One other rig that is sometimes used when squatt fishing, especially
on those few occasion when wind is a problem is the use of the very
fine Image Balsa antennas, fished bottom end only on a long line to
hand (see fig. 12). This is a very effective method when you are unable
to present the bait properly by using conventional pole fishing tactics.
Similar methods can also be employed when the wind effects your presentation on still waters. On wider canals where the far bank is just a few

metres beyond maximum pole reach, a light waggler or balsa antenna float can be used in this way to reach the edge of the far ledge. By having 3 or 4 metres of line above the float the tackle can be flicked over into position. This allows you to use a much smaller float than you would need to use to reach the same distance on the running line. Also the risk of over casting is also eliminated. Once a fish is hooked the pole can be pushed over a roller behind you and unshipped at the point where the fish can be swung in to hand or netted.

Q. *When you get to your peg, how do you go about assessing your swim? What would be your initial fishing and feeding tactics, and how would these vary to suit conditions and the use of different baits.*

Wayne: As we have mentioned in the last chapter, the important thing is to do your homework. It is essential to know what the current form is with regard to methods and baits. This can obviously vary from venue to venue. Even different sections of a venue can vary, particularly in the winter months when the fish will shoal up in different areas.

You also need to know which are the current match winning species. Again this can vary at different times of the year. In summer it may be chub or bream, in the winter it can change when the bream stop feeding and match winning weights can be made up with roach or gudgeon, with the odd bonus chub deciding the final placings, so it is very important to know the current form before deciding upon your match plan.

In the summer months, most match plans will centre around the use of squatt and pinkie tactics in the main channel, with two basic lines, one close in and the other at the bottom of the far ledge. At the same time a few casters will be put over on top of the far shelf in the hope of connecting with a few bonus fish in the latter stages of the match. On some of the wider, deeper stretches with a reasonable head of larger fish, hemp and caster tactics may also be used in the main channel as well as on the far ledge. Again knowledge of current form and local tactics are important when assessing your match plan.

Bloodworm and joker fishing can also be an effective summer method on many canals where it is allowed and early in the season the continental approach of an initial heavy bombardment of ten or fifteen balls of groundbait laced with jokers can be very effective. As the season wears on this approach may need to be modified, using a reduced opening bombardment and topping up the swim periodically with small balls of joker and leam.

In the winter months when boat traffic is reduced and the risk of the bait being dispersed by the wash of the boats or the continual changing of flow direction is reduced, drip feeding of jokers and leam throughout the match is the normal method. One very effective method of picking up a few bonus bigger fish from the far shelf during both winter and summer is to put across a good sized ball of neat jokers over on the top of the far shelf. These methods will be described in greater detail in the chapter on bloodworm fishing.

Don: On a canal you have basically got four pegs, four places where you can feed and fish:- the inside line, down the middle of the track, at the bottom of the far shelf and right across on top of the far shelf. I always feed all four lines and I think that it is easier to fish a canal than a river. Invariably on the narrower canals it is seldom windy, they nearly always have a calmness about them and those obvious features such as shelves, ledges and overhanging cover on the far bank make for obvious fish holding areas so they are easier to read.

With regards to the different methods. On many canals where blood-worm is barred, the squatt and pinkie method is very effective for roach and skimmers if the canal contains a reasonable head of fish. When I first started to use the method I was surprised just how many squatts were needed during the course of a match when a good area was drawn. In the winter I expected to use about a ½ pint but in fact I found that often I was getting through 1½ pints on a good day, and in a shallow canal this is a lot of bait when you consider just how many thousands of squatts there are in 1½ pints of bait. In the summer you can often get through twice this amount. Once you have got the fish going it seems that the more you feed the more fish you catch.

You do need to be very careful with how much groundbait you use. We often start by using a bit of Van den Eynde Supercup mixed very sloppy but once the fish have been attracted we often cut back on this and just feed neat squatts. The rig we use is a strung-out Styl rig with 8 to 10 Styls down the line and a size 24 Drennan caster blue hook (see fig. 13). You need plenty of Styl weights down the line because if the canal starts to move these need to be bunched to ensure that the flow is picked up by the tackle and the bait presented properly at the speed of the flow (see fig. 14).

When the fish are feeding really well and the bigger skimmers start to show, a deadly method is to use a fluorescent 'disco' pinkie on the hook in conjunction with the loose fed squatts and a few pinkies, alternating with double squatt as the hookbait. When things are really hard you may need to cut back on the feed and fish a single squatt on a size 26 hook. It is important whenever the bite rate slows down to keep moving the Style leads around, varying your presentation and depth to try to keep the fish coming.

Whilst all of this is going on, a few casters will have been fed over on the top of the far ledge so that later on in the match if the squatt lines die off, a few bonus fish may be picked up in the last hour. I prefer

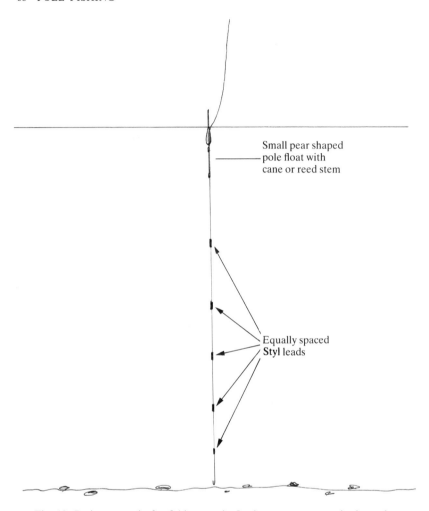

Fig. 13. Basic squatt rig for fishing canals. In deeper water more leads need to be used.

to put these over by using a pole feeding cup clipped to the end of the pole and pushed out across to the far side. (see fig. 15) This allows for the casters to be accurately placed in a much tighter area than if they are catapulted across.

Often at the start of a match, particularly if the canal contains chub, I will have a couple of casts across to the top of the far shelf, without feeding first, in the hope of picking up a couple of bonus fish in the

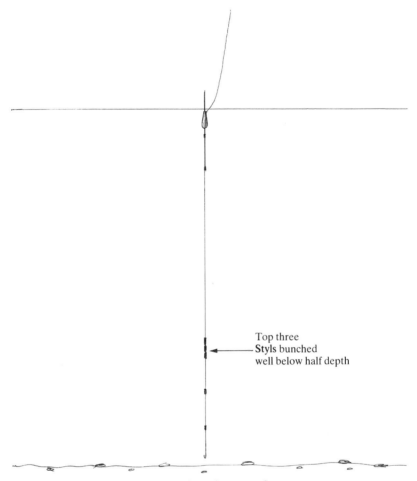

Top three
Styls bunched
well below half depth

Fig. 14. Bunching down to allow the rig to pick up any flow

first few minutes of the match. If no bites are forthcoming after a couple of casts I will then put in a few casters and leave that line completely alone until the last hour of the match, concentrating my efforts on the other lines.

Wayne: I usually like to have a sortie around to establish just what fish I have got in the swim before commiting myself to a particular baiting programme, especially on a venue that I am not too familiar with. The nature of the match has a lot to do with establishing your initial tactics.

Fig. 15. Feeding cup clipped to end of pole

In an individual event you need to go all out for the match winning species and you will generally commit yourself to a particular approach with these in mind. In a team match you tactics will be completely different. You have got to put some fish into the net early on, so as the smaller fish are easier to catch than the larger ones these will be initial priority. Even so, your approach will be a lot more cautious than when fishing as an individual.

In any canal you will only have a certain number of fish in your swim so you need to assess the best means of catching the maximum amount in the time available. In a mixed species venue it can often pay to go all out and catch as many small fish as possible in the first couple of hours, knowing that the far lines can be capitalised for the bigger fish later on, but if larger fish are few and far between it then pays to string out the catching of the smaller fish over a longer period, by using a more cautious approach. In this way you will probably catch perhaps up to half as many again, but it will take you twice as long to do it. If by doing this you find in the latter stages that you are still catching fairly regularly, then it will be foolish not to stick to it. By going over the far side for a few bonus big fish that may not materialise, you could lose your advantage and allow the other anglers to catch you up. If on the other hand your other lines have completely dried up, then you have nothing to lose and everything to gain if the bigger fish do show.

Q. *How do you cope with the constant changes in flow direction and disturbance caused by boat traffic?*

Don: Boats are a problem but they are the price we have to pay for the vast improvements that have taken place over the last ten years or so to the overall clearing out and maintenance of the canal system. But for boating interests many of the canals would still be silted up and choked with weed.

Surprisingly it is the more considerate boaters who cause the most problems from an angler's point of view. When they see a line of anglers they pull over to the far side of the channel so as to cause what they consider to be the least disturbances, not realising that in most cases this is where you are concentrating your feed and fishing. If they kept to the middle of the track they would create less of a problem. On hard days they can sometimes bring a swim alive by helping to stir up the feed and slightly colour up the water. Often when this happens you will start to catch a few fish where before you could not get a bite. Where the real problems occur is when a boat comes through quite fast and the propellor lifts a lot of the bottom silt up making the water go the colour of chocolate. This is often the kiss of death and the only thing you can do is to sit back and let things settle down and then start the building up process all over again. Often this may have to be done in a completely different area of the peg if the disturbance has been particularly severe.

Apart from this, the main problem as far as the angler is concerned is the continual changes in flow rate and flow direction caused by the movement of the boats through the locks and bridge narrows. This causes the water to push and pull in opposite directions making it very difficult to concentrate both the feed and the fish. Where possible I try not to feed when this water movement occurs, but on some days where it is happening all day long then obviously you do need to put something in, so you just have to try to judge where the feed is going.

Wayne: A lot depends upon your catch rate; if I was catching a lot of fish I would still keep feeding even though the water is moving about, providing of course that the fish still responded. But if I had only been catching the odd one or two then I would err on the side of caution and make a conscious effort not to feed until it settled down again.

On those occasions where I do feel I need to keep feeding, I do obviously try to time and position the feed so that it hits the bottom in more or less the same area each time. Unfortunately one of the most fundamental principles of angling generally takes over at this point— Sods Law. You can virtually guarantee that as the feed leaves your hand or catapult after allowing for the direction and rate of flow of the water, that before it hits the surface the canal will suddenly start to move in the opposite direction. This is the same rule that generally applies when bream fishing. After two or three biteless hours you think to yourself 'I will just put one in' and just as you have loaded a ball of groundbait into the cup of the catapult, the rod tip pulls round and you miss it!

With regard to boat disturbance, this will either help or hinder you depending upon conditions. The only consolation is that generally it is the same for everybody. Having said that, I remember the time on this year's Super League semi final on the Oxford Canal. Both Steve Pierpoint and myself were fishless after several hours of the match. The water was gin clear and the anglers around us had all been catching odd tiny perch and roach with the odd gudgeon, so you could say we were being hammered. Then a boat came through, clouding up the water as it went past. We then both started to catch gudgeon and they were big gudgeon. They were fizzing away like mad on the bottom, and we caught steadily whilst the water remained cloudy but as the match went on and the water began to clear again the bites started to slow down. Fortunately, for some strange reason, the anglers who had previously been catching stopped catching at this point and we were able to pull ahead and win the section. This just demonstrates the uncertain nature of canal fishing. It really does tax your skills and temperament.

Q. *How do your tactics vary when fishing the larger, wider canals such as the Gloucester Canal and the Stainforth and Keadby Canal etc?*

Wayne: Most of these larger canals do contain a good head of quality fish, but due to the width they do present problems that you do not normally have to contend with on the narrower canals. The biggest of these problems is wind. Often this wind is either downstream or in your face and this makes it very difficult to feed the far side of the canal properly.

Most stretches contain chub and 90% of these will be caught over on the far side and due to the width of the canals, pole tactics for these species is out of the question. The normal method is to start off by fishing the waggler, or in rough conditions a small feeder across the canal, but at the same time feeding a caster or squatt line down the middle of the channel which you will normally fish with the pole.

Often a few quick chub, if present, can be caught at the beginning, then when they have gone off you concentrate your fishing on the pole line for the roach and skimmers. Every now and then you will go back over to the far side, picking up the odd bonus fish, but generally you will concentrate on building up the pole line and the bulk of your catch will come from this.

Don: When we first started to fish the Stainforth and Keadby Canal we did not know very much about it. We were told it was a waggler job across the far side for chub and roach and so we concentrated on this. Only after a couple of visits did we realise that there were an awful lot of roach and skimmers to be caught down the middle on the pole and had we known this at first we would have been in the prize money on those early matches.

Now when we fish it we always feed both lines, alternating between them as the catch rate dictates, resting the far line and switching to the pole line as the bite rate slows, periodically going back over to the far side throughout the match. The size of roach on this canal is very good and double figure catches are quite possible using squatts and pinkies on the pole line. On some stretches the volume of chub is also quite high, so you cannot ignore the far line for long if these are about, as some of them are quite big fish.

This is a classic example of how pole tactics can be used to advantage in conjunction with the running line, a point often overlooked by many anglers who on occasions become too preoccupied with pole fishing to the exclusion of other methods. Pole fishing can become very addictive and anglers must keep an open mind on certain venues or they will often slip up.

Wayne: One quick point about feeding on these canals. I never put more than a dozen maggots over to the far side at any one time. A pouchful of maggots is the kiss of death on these waters.

I often put in a few balls of groundbait and squatts on the pole line at the beginning of the match, and then loose feed them during the rest of the match, but I never put any groundbait over to the far side.

In very windy conditions when it is impossible to hold a float across I will use a light bomb rig with a longish tail, but where possible I will always loose feed the bait across. Due to the depth of the water, particularly on the Gloucester Canal, I will use a much heavier rig than is normal on canals but the terminal tackle will always be as fine as possible. On the other canals, if the depth is only around 6 or 7 ft, in favourable conditions I will always start off with strung out Styl leads, but in deeper water or in windy conditions the more stable olivette rig is favourite.

Pole Fishing on Rivers

Q. *A lot has been written in previous books on pole fishing about still water and canal methods, but as we outlined at the beginning of this book, the pole is now being used effectively on flowing water. How do you recognise when the use of pole methods is going to give you an advantage over the running line, and perhaps more importantly, when do you use the pole in conjunction with the running line methods to give you an added advantage?*

Wayne: Wherever you fish on a river, if the wind is right for fishing a stickfloat you must also consider setting a pole up as well, providing you have a workable depth of water. Anything over 3½ to 12 ft, with a steady rate of flow is normally considered workable. I always start off with a stickfloat, plumbing the depth and running it through to establish the nature of the swim. You will be looking for any snags or variations in depth and these will then influence which particular line you will start to feed and fish. Once this is established you will then rig up the pole to suit the depth and the distance at which you are going to fish.

As to what part the pole will play on the day, this is really down to trial and error and the response of the fish during the course of the match. If things go right and the fish can be brought up to where you want them then the pole is going to be far superior, as your presentation can be controlled much better and the fish can be played out much more quickly. Your turn round time between casting and landing fish is also much quicker, so overall everything is going to be to your advantage.

On some days it will not work so well. Sometimes the fish will be reluctant to move up into pole range and you will need to go well down the swim to catch them, but fortunately this situation is the exception rather than the rule and providing the depth and flow allows you to feed them up into pole range they will usually move up eventually and once this happens your catch rate will be speeded up dramatically. You do get those days when they will come up for so long and then drop back down again and you are forever chopping and changing between the pole and the stickfloat all day long, but providing you are aware of what is happening and adjust your feeding pattern accordingly you will be able to keep catching steadily.

The method can be used just as effectively in both winter and summer. In the summer on some venues you can get away with using groundbait and on these occasions the pole really does come into its own. In the winter you are looking more to loose feeding tactics, but providing the depth and flow allows it the fish can be brought up to where you want them.

Usually, under normal conditions a rig that carries ¾ to 1¼ grammes is normally sufficient in most pole fishing situations and generally this will be fished slightly overdepth and you will continually vary the rate at which you put it through the swim until you find out how the fish want it. This is one of the great advantages of using a pole. The float can be held back or allowed to run through at various points along the swim without the rig swinging in off line, as often happens with a stickfloat, particularly if the wind is a bit tricky.

Don: You can vary the presentation far more with a pole in the first half of your peg than you can ever achieve with the running line. It is just a great way of getting bites. Often you can drop it in just in front of you, hold back whilst the tackle settles down, and as you let it go to trot through the swim you just know that you are going to get a bite. You try to do the same with a stickfloat and as you are holding back, it starts creeping round and you know the presentation is wrong.

On other occasions you find that you are struggling on the pole and despite moving your shots about the bites are few and far between. Often when this happens, you try the stick float and as the float goes a yard or so past the trotting limit of your pole tackle, the float goes under every time and you start to bag up.

You then realise that the fish have been lying just out of pole range so you modify the feeding by baiting further upstream to try to bring the fish up to within pole range. Often, if this is successful and when you switch back to the pole again things are even better.

There have been other days when despite altering the position of our feeding the fish have stayed in the bottom half of the peg and refused to be moved. On these days the use of the pole is out of the question. One of the biggest frustrations of stickfloat fishing is when the fish came too far up the swim and end up feeding directly in front of you. It is almost impossible to present the bait properly and hit the bites and there is the very real danger of the fish moving past you and into the next peg. Now with the pole this disadvantage becomes a bonus as the tackle can be brought under control at this point and bites can easily be hit. Even so, if this does happen it can still pay to modify the feeding to try to move the fish a yard or so downstream to reduce the risk of them going past you.

Q. *What are the basic types of rigs that you use for flowing waters and how do you assess your swim and decide which to use under the various conditions? What changes do you make to keep in touch with the fish?*

Wayne: Under normal conditions I like to use a float of around 1 gramme capacity. This is usually one of the inverted pear shaped type with the thickest part of the body at the top and preferably with a cane stem (see fig. 16). Initially most of the shot will be bunched in the lower half of the tackle with two or three small droppers. I like to use Styl leads, but the larger sizes above size 12 are now illegal, so I usually use non-toxic No 6's with smaller Styl leads or dust shot as the droppers. Obviously the position of the bulk shot can be varied to suit the response of the fish and it can also be strung out and spaced up the line if I want to fish a slower drop. The important thing is to keep ringing the changes until you find how the fish want the bait presented.

On deeper waters I invariably bunch up the bulk shot to get the bait down quickly to the fish and generally speed up the catch rate. On shallower water then I normally start with them spaced out for taking fish on the drop. Basically you are fishing the stick float style, but with a bristle float, and under the right conditions the pole allows you to fish it far more effectively than you can with the running line.

Obviously as well as having the length of pole to control the tackle, you are also able to use much finer line and hooks, essential when the going gets really hard and the fish are not feeding readily. For most of my river fishing now I use an 0.08 mm mainline and a 0.06 mm hook-length and this will only be 6 in long to allow for a quick replacement if I get snagged or need to change the hook size. As I mentioned in the earlier chapter on line and hooks, if a shoal of bigger fish do move in and the river bed is snag free, I will often tie a hook directly onto the main line to enable me to play them out quicker and minimise the risk of being broken.

Don: This basic approach is the same as is used by most top anglers when pole fishing on rivers. It has been arrived at by years of trial and error and although it may appear to be simple and basic, this is the real beauty of it. Complicated rigs may look impressive, with dozens of shots or Styls strategically placed up the line, but they are no more effective and should you pull out of a fish, which often happens, the whole lot will fly back and end up in an unholy tangle.

It is not the rigs that give a top angler the edge, it is the efficient

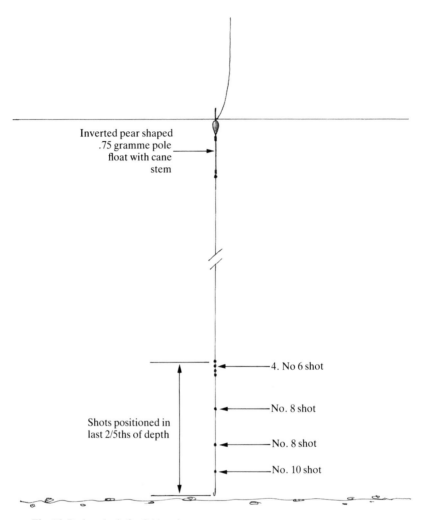

Fig. 16. Basic pole rig for fishing rivers

tackle handling and feeding patterns, combined with constant depth changing and the moving of shots around to keep the fish coming.

Practice and experience helps you to identify what is happening under the surface of the water and tells you subconsciously what changes need to be made in response. These are the real secrets of success. It all boils down to knowledge and work rate.

With regard to pole handling on flowing water, we always start off, conditions allowing, with the tackle set at 6 or 7 metres to hand, but with the rest of the pole conveniently placed so that sections can be added on as and when they are required. You need to add these at various times, for various reasons. Often, if the fish move back down the swim, you can, by adding on the sections as the tackle reaches its limit of the trot on the 6 metre length, feed the longer pole out to allow the tackle to trot over a much longer length of the swim. A very long length of swim can be covered by using this method. On other occasion you can add on sections to allow you to fish further out, say on the 9 or 10 metre line. You often need to do this when you have been catching steadily on the 6 metre line but bites slow off as the fish move out or that line needs resting. The other occasion is when you hook a big fish such as a chub or bream and your elastic is being stretched to its limit. By adding on these spare sections you can follow the fish out and reduce the risk of being broken, then as the fish begins to tire you can feed the pole back gradually, removing the sections as you go.

In all of these instances you seldom put on or take off sections one at a time. You normally clip on a length of two or three sections and feed it backwards or forwards as required. With experience and practice this can be done smoothly and efficiently. Normally we will always feed two stick float and pole lines—one at 6 or 7 metres and one at 9 or 10 metres, alternating betweem them during the course of the match as and when we feel that one particular line needs resting. Often we will also feed a waggler line further out if we feel that this method is likely to have a role to play at some time during the match, but it is important to always keep these lines regularly fed throughout the match, even though you may end up by not fishing them all.

Wayne: Yes you do need to keep working, moving shots about, changing depth and also you need to vary the rate at which you put the float through in relation to the flow of the river. On light to moderate flows the rig we have mentioned will cover most of the situations you are likely to encounter from catching on the drop, running through with the speed of the current or holding back to slow the bait down evenly, or when you want to check the float and lift the tail at various points in the swim.

In heavier flows or where the river is carrying extra water a round bodied float used in conjunction with an olivette can be a very effective method, particularly when the fish want the bait slowed down but held near the bottom (see fig. 17). The wide shoulder at the top of the float prevents the body from rising up out of the water as the tackle is being held back and the olivette prevents the bait being lifted too far up off the bottom. Often, especially during the winter months we will have two

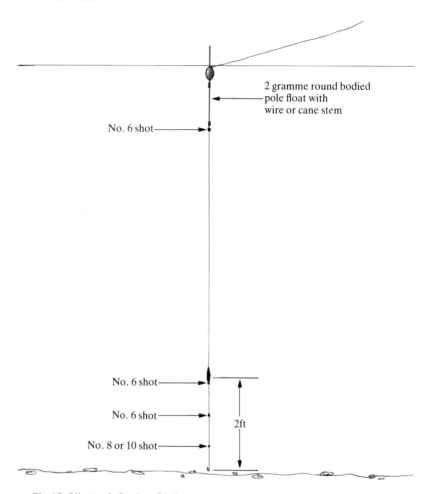

2 gramme round bodied
pole float with
wire or cane stem

No. 6 shot

No. 6 shot

No. 6 shot

No. 8 or 10 shot

2ft

Fig. 17. Olivette rig for deep flowing water

poles set up, one with a standard rig and one with an olivette rig. This allows us to keep varing the presentation as and when we need to.

Often you need to vary the feeding, not only the amount and regularity of the feed, but the timing as well.

Different species react in different ways to your loose feed. For roach and bream the traditional method of casting then feeding on a little and often basis is the usual method. Sometimes you may feed just once at the beginning of the trot, on other occasions you may feed two or three

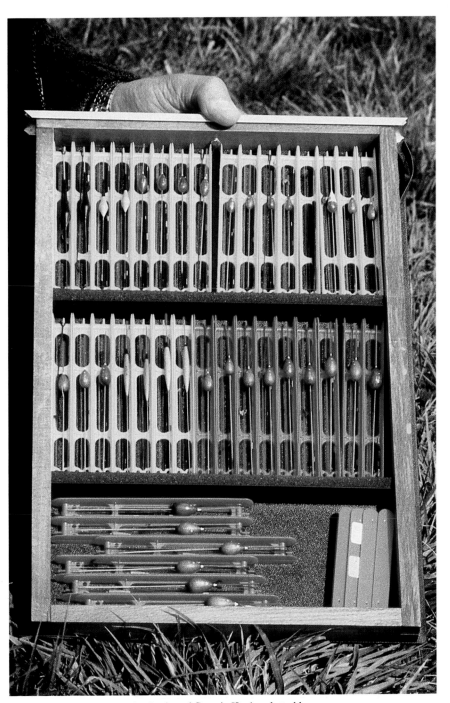

A selection of Captain Ken's pole tackles.

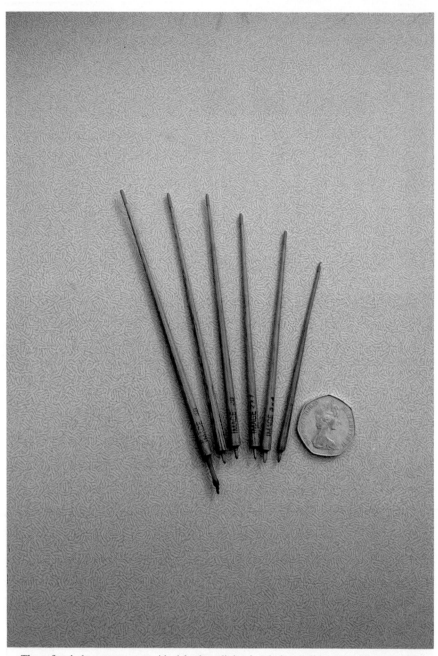

These fine balsa antennae are ideal for long-lining in windy conditions on stillwaters and canals.

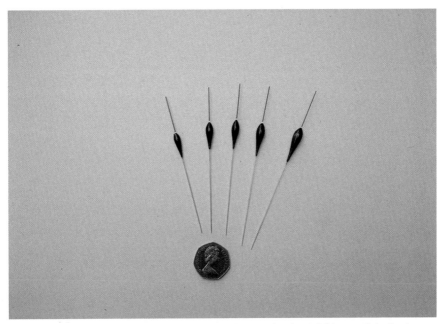

These delicate cane-stemmed floats are ideal for 'on the drop' fishing on light-flowing rivers.

Cane-stemmed 'Team England' pole floats, Wayne's favourite pattern for fishing the Trent.

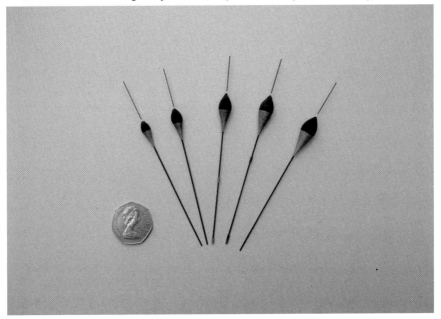

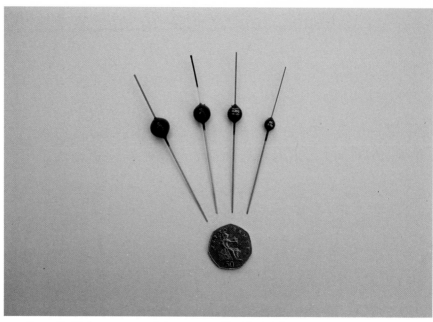

Round-bodied cane-stemmed river pattern; ideal for holding back with an Olivette rig.

These heavy wire-stemmed floats are also used in conjunction with an Olivette whilst running through on rivers.

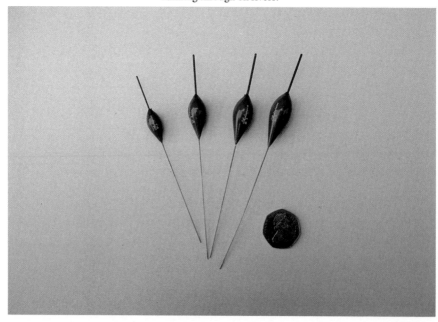

Don swings in another Long Higgin skimmer on his 'Superteam' whip. Note the efficient tackle layout.

Top-quality bronze maggots, currently the modern match angler's first choice of bait.

Fresh casters—a deadly canal bait.

A sample of the continental groundbaits now very much in favour.

Wayne hangs on to 11 metres of pole in the rowing course at Holme Pierrepont.

Releasing the clips at the bottom of the Steadfast Protectanet.

Fish being released out of bottom of net into the weighing net.

times during each trot, keeping a constant trickle of feed going down all of the time.

With some species such as dace or chub a different approach is called for. Often it pays to put in a bunch of feed, then cast on top of it so that the hookbait is going down the swim with the loose feed. The fish will often dive into this bunch of feed, snapping up as much as possible but ignoring odd single items that are drifted down to them. How many times have you caught a chub and it has spewed out a mass of maggots as you are unhooking it? Obviously it has been diving into a bunch of loose fed maggots, snapping them up as fast as it can, then ignoring the odd single maggot on the hook as it is busily digesting them before the next lot comes down.

Obviously, if your hook bait is not amongst that bunch of bait it is unlikely to be taken. This is why many anglers only catch 5 or 6 lbs of roach and an odd chub when they actually have 20 lbs of a potential chub weight in their peg. By being aware of the habits of the various species you can adjust your rhythm accordingly to take advantage of them as and when they arrive.

Generally though this is less of a problem when using a pole than it is when using a stick float. The longer length allows you to place the tackle exactly where you want it, so you can cast in, feed, pull the tackle back over the feed and then let it go down with it. Obviously if you try to do this with the running line you need to cast well past your line to allow you to pull the tackle back, but often when it is windy you are not always able to do it with sufficient accuracy or at the distance you require. You just do not have the same degree of control.

When feeding for the pole, your feed needs to be placed with much more accuracy and generally in a much tighter area. With the running line you can usually cast around a yard further or a yard shorter as the fish move about, but with the pole you do tend to go down the same line all of the time unless you add on extra sections, so you cannot allow the feed to be spread out over a wide area.

Due to the limited distance you are able to trot down the swim you must also ensure that the feed gets down to the bottom within this distance and this can often mean feeding slighly upstream of you. This is fine whilst the fish are feeding on or near the bottom, but if they show signs of coming up in the water for the feed you must progressively start to feed further downstream to prevent the risk of them moving past you.

The way you play the fish is also important, particularly when pole fishing. It is very easy to get carried away when using the pole, as the elastic does tend to pump them up and out of the water very quickly. When using the automatically running line you do tend to allow them to drop back and then play them gently sideways away from the shoal, causing the minimum of disturbance, and you should always try to make

Wayne netting a plump Trent skimmer

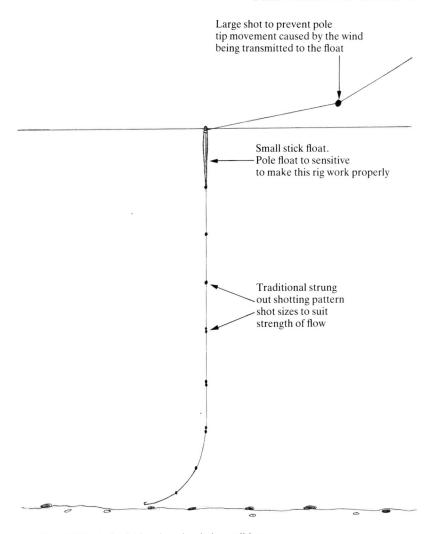

Large shot to prevent pole
tip movement caused by the wind
being transmitted to the float

Small stick float.
Pole float to sensitive
to make this rig work properly

Traditional strung
out shotting pattern
shot sizes to suit
strength of flow

Fig. 18. Pole rig for fishing rivers in windy conditions

a conscious effort to do the same when pole fishing. By lifting the fish
straight up and out of the area where you have hooked it you risk spooking
the rest of the fish and make it harder to keep them feeding where you
want them which is just downsteam of you. This often happens to us
and we know it is wrong and it can be very difficult forcing ourselves
to think and slow it down a bit, especially when we are on a shed full.

With the smaller species such as gudgeon it does not seem to matter so much, but with the larger more wary species it can make a big difference to the long term catch rate.

Don: As we have already mentioned, the pole can also save you a lot of time. Obviously you save the time taken to reel in the tackle when you need to re-cast or examine and change your hookbait, but also you can save a lot of time by not having to re-cast between biteless trots down the swim. If you are fishing 11 metres of pole with 5 or 6 metres of line, you can initially cast it into the swim, mending the line and straightening out the tackle and let it do down. But if you do not get a bite you do not necessarily have to bring it all out and re-cast. You can just pull it back up to the head of the swim and let it run through again, saving the time needed to re-cast and for the tackle to get down to the depth again. This is one of the beauties of pole fishing, particularly when using maggot as bait. Obviously, you know that if you have not had a bite the bait will still be on the hook and in a serviceable condition. Also, if bites are coming regularly from a certain part of the swim you can cast to and manouver the tackle so that it gets to that point in the minimum of time and know that when it does you will have immediate control over it. This is a big time saver and saving time anywhere possible is a most essential part of match fishing.

Q. *How do you cope with extreme conditions such as strong downstream winds and floods?*

Wayne: In very windy conditions it is obviously impossible to hang on to a really long length of pole. Often you will have to use a shorter pole than you would like, but normally you can feed the fish into the line you are able to fish comfortably and although you may not be catching as quickly, you are able to present the bait reasonably well and catch at a better rate than by using the running line under the same conditions. You can improve things by using a back shot and sinking the pole tip under the water and although this means you cannot strike as cleanly due to the cushioning effect of the water on the pole tip, a reasonable degree of success can normally be achieved.

Sometimes you may need to go to the extreme of putting a large B.B. or A.A.A. shot midway between the pole tip and the float tip to prevent the sway of the pole tip jerking the tackle, particularly when the fish want the bait put through slower than the flow of water and you need to hold back. On these occasions I would normally switch to using a standard stick float as opposed to a bristle float as the presence of this large shot can interfere with the delicate setting of the bristle (see fig. 18).

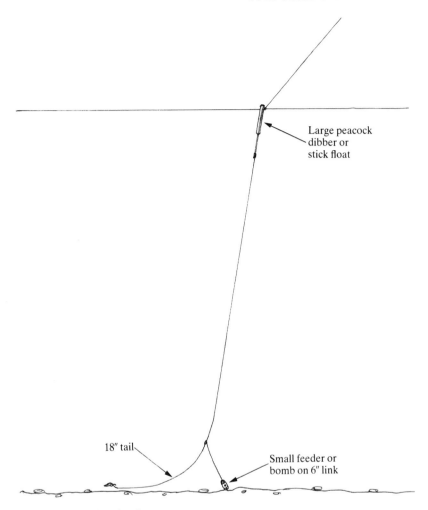

Large peacock
dibber or
stick float

18″ tail

Small feeder or
bomb on 6″ link

Fig. 19. Float legering rig

In flooded conditions you may often need to overshot the rig to allow you to hold back on to the tackle without the body pulling up out of the water, inching the tackle through well over depth. You will get a lot of false bites doing this but with practise you can identify these and as long as it means you are putting some fish in the net it is a price you are prepared to pay.

On those occasion when the river is well up and coloured and the fish want the bait laid hard on, the pole does allow you to position the bait at any distance out up to the maximum length of the pole using float leger tactics. We had a lot of success with this method in the Winter League matches on the tidal Trent and once mastered it can be a very effective method.

Normally a large flat topped stick float is used in conjunction with a Arlesey bomb or a link or swan shots fished paternoster style. (see fig. 19) The tackle is set slightly overdepth and dropped in gently and the setting of the float tip is governed by the position of the pole tip which is held above the float on a short line, slightly upstream. The benefit of using swan shots is that if the weights get caught up in the rocks you are able to pull it clear due to the line sliding through the shots. A stronger main line of up to 2–3 lbs B.S. is usually preferable in these conditions.

Don: This is a good method. A bomb link of about 6 in is normally used in conjunction with an 18 in tail. Providing the bottom is reasonably snag free, a small block end feeder that just takes a dozen maggots can be also used in place of the bomb, or one of those small line feeders can be used, slid onto the link above the bomb or swan shots. A large peacock dibber can also be used instead of a stick float. They are very light but also buoyant and are ideal for this particular job. Years ago, anglers could only dream of being able to lay on at the sort of range now allowed by modern poles. They had to resort to the quiver tip under extreme conditions and were forever being snagged up as the current pulled the tackle around into the rocks. It takes a bit of practice to get everything balanced right but once the method is mastered it can be deadly.

Whip Fishing

Q. *The last couple of seasons has seen the introduction and large scale use of carbon whips, used in conjunction with long line tactics for speed fishing on all types of waters. What features do you look for in a good whip?. What is your approach to whip fishing on the various waters and what differences are there in the terminal tackle used?. How does your approach vary for the different species such as roach, gudgeon and bleak?.*

Wayne: Whenever the target species are smaller fish up to 8 oz in weight and they can be brought to within whip range, I always prefer to use a whip rather than a pole. They are a lighter tool to use and the new carbon whips have a firm, but forgiving action well suited to this type of fishing. Length for length they are much slimmer than a pole making for easier handling and the extra action allows for the use of lighter floats and tackles on those occasions when it is necessary to use them. Most of the major tackle firms now have a good range of carbon whips available and the main consideration when choosing a whip is the degree of stiffness in the tip. For canal use where fine lines and hooks are necessary, then a fine soft tip is needed to balance this and prevent cracking off when the odd decent fish is encountered. When river fishing or when speed fishing, heavier tackle is essential, combined with a stiffer tip to keep the right balance. Often when gudgeon fishing we will use 1 lb or if possible 1½ lb hooklengths, combined with the largest hook we can get away with which often will be as large as a fine wire size 16, particularly when river fishing with maggot as the hookbait. This kind of tackle can be comfortably used with quite a strong tip, essential for getting the larger gudgeon up and out of the water in the twinkling of an eye. With a fine soft tip you end up having to play them out, which is wrong if a big weight of these fish is to be attained. The heavier line will also allow you to cope with the odd bonus fish that may come along, but also it helps to prevent accidents if the swim has the odd snag. You cannot afford for a breakage to upset your rhythm and under most speed fishing situations which occur, and when the fish are feeding freely the heavier tackle will not put them off.

Often, the cheaper whips are more suited to this heavier work as they tend to be that bit thicker and stiffer than the more expensive ones. The important thing, as when you consider any item of tackle, is to take into account the type of fishing you intend to be doing and buy the right type of whip to cope most efficiently with it. If you find you will be fishing various venues and styles then a couple of whips, a stiff one and a fine one will be needed to cope with these various situations. The important thing to remember is that there is no such thing as a good all round whip.

Don: Wayne is right, you do need different tools for different jobs. Often when we fish the rivers such as the Avon or the Trent, we will be catching anything from 1 oz gudgeon to 6 oz roach and skimmers at a very high rate, using 1 lb or 1½ lb bottoms. If a fine canal type whip was used under these circumstances your catch rate would be slowed down too much due to the length of time it takes to play the fish out. It is surprising just how much pressure you can put on a fish using a strong tip and 1 lb line. On a canal where the size of fish is very small and due to the type of bait such as bloodworm, pinkies or squatts you need to use fine tackle, then a fine soft whip is essential. Really it is relative to the size of fish you are catching and the rate of which you need to get them out.

The main advantage that fishing to hand with a whip gives you over the pole is speed. Having an efficient tackle layout and getting into a smooth rhythm is essential. Everything needs to be at hand so that you can concentrate on the job of catching as many fish as possible in the shortest possible time. Normally I always wear a bait apron and have my keep net strategically placed in front of me so that I can unhook a fish and drop it into the net without looking. This also helps to catch the odd fish that drops off the hook as you swing it into you. A large net with an expanding top ring is useful for this purpose.

Bait changes are also kept to a minimum, often we are still catching fish on just the skins if everything is working right.

The rigs we use are usually similar to our normal pole rigs. Lighter versions of the strung out Style lead rigs are used for taking fish on the drop or from around the surface areas of the water, but surprisingly we will use heavier rigs for gudgeon fishing and this applies to canal fishing as well as on the rivers. A 1.25 gramme float used in conjunction with an olivette or a length of tungsteon tubing is the usual starting rig. The olivette or main weight is normally about 6″ above the hook with a No. 8 dropper, but on occasions you can have the olivette just 3″ from the hook with no drop shot at all. In these situations the fish will be feeding really well with the float going under almost immediately

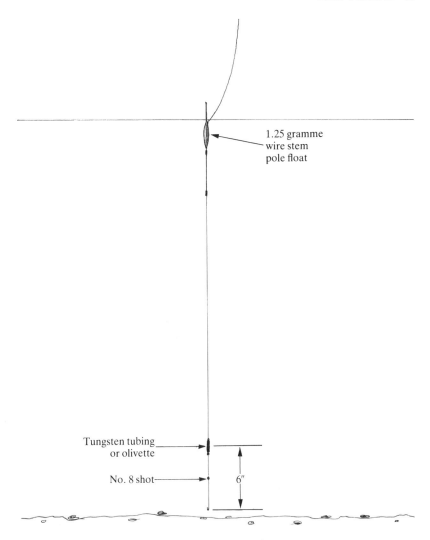

Fig. 20. Gudgeon fishing rig for both rivers and canals

the float cocks. The rig is always fished 1—1½" off the bottom, so very accurate plumbing of the depth is essential. (See fig: 20).

Wayne: In most cases, whether you are fishing on a canal or a river, the gudgeon are found in 3 or 4 ft of water and the bottom needs to be very flat and even. Tremendous weights of these fish were being caught towards the end of the 1989–90 season on the river Trent in this type of swim, using loose fed maggot tactics. The gudgeon being caught were of a large average size from 1 oz up to 1½ oz in some places. Gudgeon tactics on the canals are quite different. The same basic rig described by Don is still used, but in conjunction with bloodworm or squatts and pinkies where bloodworm is banned. But where it is allowed the bloodworm is the premier bait for gudgeon on canals. Where possible we use a size 22 or 20 fine wire hook, only going down to a size 24 when things get really hard. The hooklengths will be only ¾ lb b.s. for canal fishing and the average size of fish will be much smaller than on the rivers.

When fishing on the drop for roach or other small fish we like to use a small dibber or thin piece of peacock quill fished bottom end only. When speed fishing with light shotting down the line the bristle floats are very prone to spinning around and tangling which is very time consuming and far less efficient. The shots are moved about to vary the presentation just the same as in any normal fishing situation.

If the quarry is bleak, the float plays very little part as a bite indicator, as normally as soon as the bleak feels the float it will eject the bait. In ideal conditions you watch the maggot as it sinks in the water and strike when it suddenly disappears from view. If the water is cloudy or when there is a chop on the surface, this method is obviously out of the question and the usual method then is to cast in the tackle and start counting, watching the float to see how long it takes for the bite. This indicates the current level at which the fish are feeding in the water. Say the float goes under at the count of 4, on the next cast you will count to 3 and then tighten. Often you will connect with the fish and as they move up or down in the water you shorten or extend your count to suit.

It is important not to straighten out the tackle when bleak fishing as you want it to take the bait without it feeling the float. It is much better if the tackle falls in a heap. This gives the fish more time to swim around with the bait in its mouth and increases your chance of catching it. If when you lift the tackle you have not connected with the fish you immediately re-cast and repeat the procedure. Many anglers use either a small piece of hardwood or a small porcupine quill float connected onto the line with two pieces of silicon tubing. It is important that the ends of the float do not protrude out of the tubing if tangles are to be prevented. (See fig: 21).

In ideal conditions no shot is needed down the line when the fish are feeding close to the surface, but on those occasions when the fish are feeding lower down in the water, micro dust shot can be spaced evenly down the line for taking on the drop or bunched together if the fish are feeding further down and are not coming up in the water. The largest

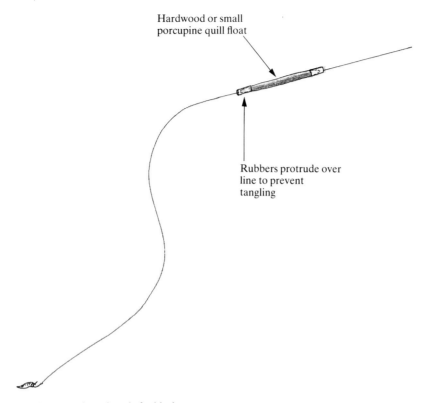

Hardwood or small
porcupine quill float

Rubbers protrude over
line to prevent
tangling

Fig. 21. Basic surface rig for bleak

hook possible should be used in conjunction with a 1–1½ lb hooklength.
The barb is normally squeezed down to speed up the unhooking process.
Top bleak anglers shake the fish off with a flick of the wrist as opposed
to unhooking them in the conventional manner.

Don: There are two main methods of connecting your tackle to the
tip. One is to use a 'magic loop' in your tackle which slides over a length
of hollow woven cord which is often connected to the tip of commercial
whips, pulling it tight above the stop knot on the cord. (See fig: 22A)
Or the second method, and the one we prefer, is to use two pieces of
silicon tubing which are slid over the tip, locking the line in place. (See
fig: 22B). Note that the length of tubing that is slid on first is shorter
than the front piece of tubing. The line is trapped by the shorter piece,
then wrapped around the pole half a dozen times, then trapped again

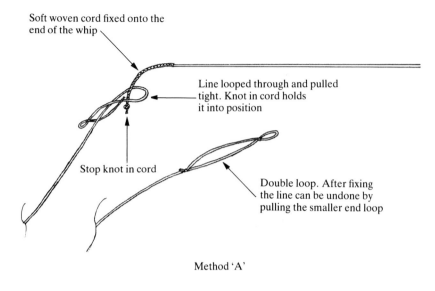

Soft woven cord fixed onto the
end of the whip

Line looped through and pulled
tight. Knot in cord holds
it into position

Stop knot in cord

Double loop. After fixing
the line can be undone by
pulling the smaller end loop

Method 'A'

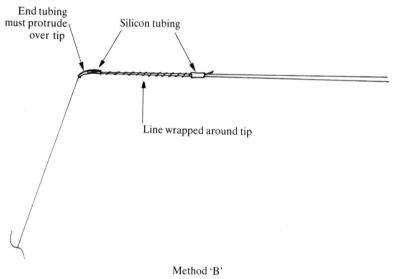

End tubing
must protrude
over tip

Silicon tubing

Line wrapped around tip

Method 'B'

Fig. 22. Two ways of fixing line to whips by the 'magic loop' for quick tackle changes
or by silicon tubing

at the tip of the pole by the longer piece. It is important to leave a small amount of this overhanging the end of the tip if tangling is to be avoided. In the old days when only glass fibre whips were available, an eye was normally attached to the tip which were normally made of hollow fibreglass and the line was attached to this. Now with the very fine solid carbon tips that we are currently using this is not practical and the two methods of attachment we have just described are much neater and far more efficient.

Bloodworm Fishing

Q. *At the top level of match fishing the use of bloodworm and jokers is essential on those venues where it is allowed and it is important for any angler who wishes to progress to the top in match fishing to have a full understanding of its effectiveness and use. What is your approach to its use on the various types of venues, and how do you go about obtaining it and keeping it in good condition?.*

Wayne: Many anglers who have read about bloodworm fishing but who have not actually used it, are generally under the impression that it is a small fish bait. This is just not so. All fish will take bloodworms, after all, it occurs naturally in still waters and is the staple diet of all fish from gudgeon to big carp. When used on waters that contain quality fish such as on the rowing course at Holme Pierrepont, it will attract all sizes and species of fish. On those occasions you can use it in the feed and fish say caster, or caster and bloodworm on the hook and still catch the bigger fish but reduce the chance of the smaller fish from getting to the hook bait first. The reason that it does catch a lot of small fish is because in most waters there are far more of them than there are big ones and when you use bloodworm on the hook, they get to it first. Having said that, on venues such as Holme Pierrepont I often have match weights of 20 to 30 lbs of fish by using bloodworm on the hook and you cannot get weights of fish like this in five hours by only catching small ones.

We are not out-and-out bloodworm anglers, but due to the wide variety of matches and venues that we need to fish as members of the Superteam, we have had to learn and master the method for on those occasions that we do need to fish it and we have all had a lot of success over the last few years, often against anglers who are considered to be traditional bloodworm men.

The actual locating and collecting of the bait has been fully covered in most of the pole fishing books that have been published in recent years so I do not want to waste space by duplicating their advice. Basically, bloodworms are found in still waters such as farm ponds and lakes with

This fine catch of bream and roach is the result of just a couple of hours pole fishing on the Holme Pierrepont rowing course with bloodworm

thick silty bottoms and jokers are found in flowing waters such as streams near sewage outfalls which also have silt bottoms. For ease of scraping these need to be weed free and clear of obstructions such as stones or boulders etc. Once you get the bait home it needs to be riddled through and cleaned so that it is completely free of weed and debris.

As jokers live in flowing water they can only be kept fresh by keeping them in water that has some form of circulation and this is achieved by using fish tank aeration pumps or by a constant light flow of fresh water. I use shallow trays that are about $2' \times 18'' \times 6''$ deep. Into these I put 4 pipes which are weighted by lead wire and connected to a fish tank pump. I drop these into the water at various points and switch on. This causes the water to circulate the jokers around in the bottom. Each tray will hold about ¾ pint of neat jokers which will just cover the bottom in a single layer. It is important not to put too many in so that they lie on top of each other. In the summer they will keep for several days providing you change the water daily and remove any dead floaters from the surface.

Another way of keeping them is to have a tray with a mesh covered hole at one end. This is placed in the shade over a drain, and water from an outside tap is allowed to trickle into the container and flow out of the hole at the other end. This ensures that a constant flow of fresh water is passing over the bait.

Bloodworm are best kept out of water in small newspaper packets with just enough damp peat mixed in with them to keep them separated. These packets are then stored in a refrigerator. It is important to lay the packets on the trays in the fridge separately and not on top of each other, or the bait will be damaged. The peat and the newspaper needs to be changed daily, or the dampness will cause the peat to go fusty and this will kill the bloodworm. During the summer months the bait will go off very quickly, particularly in really hot weather, so we always transport it to the match in freezer boxes. It is possible to buy boxes with removable trays and these are essential for laying your packets of bait out separately as you must not put the weight of one packet onto the top of another.

To transport your jokers to the match the water must be strained off and the bait gently allowed to dry off. It is then wrapped neat into small newspaper packets. Unlike bloodworm, we do not mix our jokers with peat. The packets are then laid in trays in the freezer box and once at the waterside they can be lightly sprayed with an atomising spray and sprinkled with leam. If by any chance you find the bait has started to die off whilst being transported do not be too worried. Dead jokers are just as effective as live ones, the fish still go mad for them.

Don: Most bloodworm fishing is done by using the traditional continental bottom fishing tactics with the bait fished just off the bottom. We generally use wire stemmed bristle floats in conjunction with olivettes 6″ to 12″ from the hook. When we use groundbait to introduce the jokers we normally use a mix of Van den Eynde Supercup and leam. The deeper the water, the stiffer we make the mix and this is achieved by adding a greater proportion of leam.

On bream venues where we want the groundbait to have an additional food content to keep the fish munching, a blend of Van den Eynde Secret and brown crumb is used. But for all other species the Supercup and leam combination has proved to be the most effective. Many anglers from other parts of the country have their own preferences for other makes and brands of groundbait, and many of these are equally effective, but this is what we use and it seems to work very well for us. The main attracting and fish holding ingredient is of course the jokers, the groundbait and leam is only used to get the bait down to where we want it and release it at the rate we want it to be released at. By altering the mix slightly or by squeezing some balls harder than others we can vary the way the balls break up in the water. Different waters respond to feeding in different ways and the approach on one particular water can vary at different times of the year.

Normally during the summer months most waters will take a reasonable bombardment initially and this can often be topped up later on in the match. Other waters respond best to a ball of feed being put in at regular intervals. During the winter months, particularly on clear shallow venues the joker often needs to be introduced neat or just held together with a small amount of leam. Again only experience or local knowledge of the waters can guide you as to which approach is the most productive and initially you may make some mistakes. We still make them now, but gradually a pattern will emerge and they will be kept to the minimum.

Wayne: When the fish are responding well, almost as soon as the olivette has reached the bottom the float will disappear. On other occasions, particularly during the winter months bites will need to be induced. This can often be achieved by lifting or jerking the bait a few inches up in the water and allowing it to settle again, simulating the natural movement of the bloodworm. This can often be a deadly method, producing an almost instant response from the fish. On those occasions when it does not work it normally means that either there are no fish there or they are not feeding.

Many anglers, even those who use bloodworm and jokers regularly, fail to recognise how the bait actually works in the water. Some of them are convinced that unless the bait is taken down to the bottom quickly by the groundbait it will swim off and take the fish with it. I have experimented with it and on a number of occasions when I have been fishing on very clear venues and I have put a solid ball of neat joker into the margins and watched what happens. They dive straight down to the bottom and stay there. The odd one or two do pop up from time to time but the majority stay hard on the bottom. If the bottom is soft they gradually bury themselves into the silt which is after all, where they live naturally.

I am also convinced that as they are so very fragile, when they are squeezed up in a ball of groundbait 90% of them are killed anyway. Not that this matters, if anything it probably helps, as they will still attract the fish, but as they are dead they cannot wriggle down into the silt. The important thing is that they do attract fish and stimulate them into feeding as they love the stuff, and will still feed on it when they do not want to know maggot baits.

As Don has said it can pay you to vary the mix you are using. I often put in ten really hard balls to start off with but then periodically top that up with much smaller balls, squeezed softly so they start to break up on the way down. This is I suppose a combination of traditional English feeding tactics and the continental bombardment method, but I still feel that if we could overcome our natural inhibitions about the continental approach and have the courage to try them out under match conditions we may be pleasantly surprised by the results.

I remember when last season on the river Soar the Leicester Sensas lads brought over the French champion, I cannot remember his name but he was ever such a nice lad and on this particular match I drew next to him. It was a time when we had been catching a few fish on the Soar, but when I saw him come walking down with all of his bait buckets my heart sank and I thought, 'Oh no, he's not going to fish here, is he?'. You would not believe how much bait he mixed up. It was just Sensas Magic and a bit of binder, nothing special, and he mixed something like 50 grapefruit sized balls up and all he put into it was less than ½ pint of jokers and less than ½ pint of casters which as you can imagine was totally lost in that volume of bait.

Now this part of the river Soar is gin clear and only about 5 or 6 ft deep and I thought, 'This is going to be the kiss of death'. He put 30 balls out on the 11 metre line and another 20 out on the 6 metre line. I have never seen anything like it. All I had with me was a pint of maggots to loose feed with and I thought 'Well aren't we all right here then'. Anyway, he cast in and he caught a fish on his first trot down. He was using bloodworm on the hook and that initial bombardment was all he put in for the first 3 hours.

He continued to catch steadily, then after about 3 hours the swim died off and he stopped catching. Now he knew from what the lads had told him, that if he could catch 6 or 7 lbs of fish he stood a chance of winning the match, so he fed again and caught another fish first trot down and continued to catch fish up to the end of the match. He ended up winning the section with 5 lb odd and beating me by about ½ lb which was a lot of fish on the day. When you consider that he used less than a pint of jokers all day it was an incredible performance and it proves that the fish will stand a bombardment providing it contains something that they want to eat. But also, that it can pay to make them search for it instead of giving them it all on a plate. I am sure that had the swim got the potential for a larger weight he would have put proportionally more jokers into the feed. As it was he measured its capacity exactly.

Don: On very clear shallow canals where you know the fish will not respond to groundbaiting tactics, neat jokers or bloodworm can be put over the swim and fed by using a feeding cup clipped onto the tip of the pole. When loose feeding like this the fish will often come up in the water to intercept them on the drop. In these circumstances I use a different set up to the usual olivette rig. The type of float remains the same, but instead of an olivette I use micro dust shot evenly strung out over the lower two thirds of the depth. (See fig. 23).

This rig is ideal for taking fish at all levels in the water and bites are usually positive and hittable and it is seldom that the bait will be taken without it being registered on the float. Normally when using this set up it is seldom that I will leave it for very long once the bait has reached the bottom. Normally as soon as the bait has settled I lift it back out and re-cast. The method can also be used when you are feeding soft balls of leam and jokers into the swim. Normally you use just enough leam to bind the bait for throwing and it breaks up immediately it hits the surface. On most of the narrow canals a small ball can be thrown comfortably over to the far ledge.

On most canals we will always feed two or three lines when bloodworm fishing and often we will have both of the different types of tackles set up. Often we will groundbait the middle and at the bottom of the far shelf, and drip feed jokers and leam on the inside line at the bottom of the near shelf. The olivette rig will be fished over the groundbait and the 'drop' rig is fished on the near line.

If bloodworm fishing is allowed in your area and is fished regularly on the local matches, it can pay you to go along as a spectator and see how the local anglers approach it. This will give you some idea of what volume of feed to use on that particular venue.

Wayne: As we mentioned in the chapter on hooks, we normally use either the Drennan Caster blue hooks or the Tubertini Series 2 hooks for bloodworm fishing. On canals size 24 or 22 are used with single bloodworm or a 20 or 22 for fishing double worm. If the fish are feeding really well we always use the largest hook we can get away with and if large

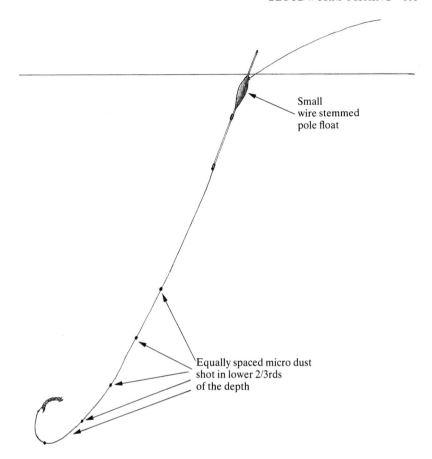

Small
wire stemmed
pole float

Equally spaced micro dust
shot in lower 2/3rds
of the depth

Fig. 23. Drop fishing rig for bloodworm

skimmers are likely we often use 2 or 3 bloodworms on a size 18. Sometimes on venues such as the rowing course at Holme Pierrepont we use
a caster or a caster and bloodworm cocktail for the larger skimmers and
quality roach. On these occaions we would usually use the stronger
Tubertini Series 2 hooks.

   The main thing to remember when you are hooking the bloodworm
is to put the hook point lightly through the greenish head of the bloodworm, and care must be taken not to squeeze the bait during the hooking
process or you will burst it. (See fig: 24) One way of doing it is to wet

Wayne displays a fine Rowing Course bream caught on a bloodworm and caster cocktail bait

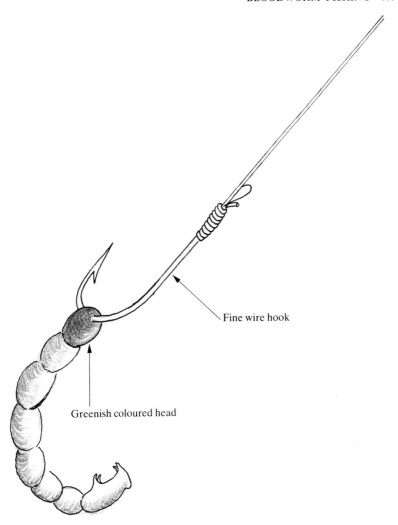

Fine wire hook

Greenish coloured head

Fig. 24. Correctly hooking a bloodworm

your finger and lay the worm along it. It will normally hold in place whilst hooking, providing your hook point is razor sharp, which it always needs to be. Some anglers lay the bloodworms out on a damp towel, laid across the knee and hook them off as they are required.

Match Experiences

Q. *Finally, to try to put all the points we have covered into perspective, I would like you to think back and tell me about any particular match, successful or otherwise where you had to make a lot of changes and adjustments to find and keep in touch with the fish, explaining what you had to do and why you did it. Also, where appropriate, what mistakes you may have made and in hindsight, how you could have perhaps improved upon your final result?.*

Wayne: One match that I think illustrates well the importance of pole fishing on a river, was one that I fished a couple of years ago on the river Trent at Burton Joyce. It was at the back end of the season and the river had been fishing particularly well, so I knew that a big weight would be needed to win the match. It was a Saturday match with a good turnout of over 120 anglers, and I drew perfectly, up near the outfall and when I arrived at the peg there was about 6″ of extra water in the river compared with mid week and there was a lot of bleak topping. I knew I would catch some roach because the colour of the water was perfect and it was a nice warm day.

With the number of bleak that were topping, I made up my mind to start by going for these, as on this stretch they are very big bleak of 1 oz plus, and a good weight can soon be put together. Later on in the match, providing the roach began to show, I would then switch to catching these on the pole and the stickfloat. I had some good anglers pegged around me so I knew that if the roach were going to show later on, then by keeping my eye on these lads I would know when to change.

The whistle went and I started off on the bleak whip and put about a hundred of these into the net in the first hour, at the same time feeding the stickfloat and pole line. I didn't look around me much in this first hour, but I wasn't conscious of any splashing of hooked fish so I kept going. After about an hour and ten minutes I noticed a few landing nets coming out so I decided to make the change to the long pole to see what was happening. As I have mentioned, I had been feeding out on the 9 metre line as well as on the 4 metre line for the bleak. I had been loose feeding bronze maggot and it was one of those rare days that when I did change over, I started catching useful sized skimmers of 3 to 4 oz apiece straight away, so they had obviously settled down and started feeding for some time. I was using a 1¼ gramme float with shots and Style leads down the line and I ended up having to bunch the leads to get through the bleak, which were beginning to be a bit of a nuisance at this time. Once I made this change it was brilliant, I was getting a skimmer a cast. Suddenly the pace of the water speeded up, probably due to an increased outlet of water from the outfall, and I lost them. I guessed that they had probably dropped down the swim a bit so I put the pole down and picked up the stickfloat rod and although it wasn't as good I was still connecting with a few fish and a few roach were beginning to show amongst the skimmers.

After a while, the pace of the water started to slow down again, so I switched back to the pole and it was solid with fish, only this time it was roach. I still had 1½ to 2 hours of the match left to go, and I was already into big double figures, so I knew it was a case of just keeping going. The other anglers around me were also catching well, but I knew that I had a 5 lb start on them with the early catch of bleak. Fortunately the roach kept coming and I also had a bonus of 6 or 7 chub, not big chub, but around 1 lb apiece, so they were very useful. In the last half an hour the peg began to die again, so I went back on the stickfloat but nothing much was happening. In desparation I put a few extra sections on to the pole and tried the 12 metre line and as luck would have it I found them again and I had a good late burst up to the final whistle. I won the match with 27 lbs, a couple of pounds ahead of the runner up, so that early start on the bleak paid dividends.

Throughout the day I kept moving the leads around on the pole float rig when the bleak allowed me to use a slower drop, bunching them heavier when I needed too. I didn't try to feed the bleak off because if you do it means that more feed will be getting through to the other fish and as I was catching as well as those around me I didn't want to risk over doing it. The fact that I was catching as well as I was meant that just enough was getting through to hold them.

I drew the same peg again a couple of weeks later, but this time the bleak were not there and I was unable to put a quick 5 lbs into the net in the first hour. I came second in the match with 19 lbs of roach and skimmers.

With regard to stillwater pole fishing, last year I entered the Wednesday league on the Rowing Course at Holme Pierrepont. Only about 50 anglers fished it but they were amongst the cream of England's top pole anglers and it was a very good series to enter, pitting my wits against these lads. I had always caught a few fish on the pole on this venue, mainly on the maggot, and I had won a few evening matches and had also done quite well on the day matches with decent weights, and I felt that the experience of fishing against them would improve my own ability.

I decided that I knew it all and that I would stick to my guns and fish the long pole with loose fed maggot and use a feeder line if I could for the odd bonus bream or for when the pole line failed to produce. I started off on the first match and this method was all wrong. The wind was blowing too hard and there was a strong undertow making it very difficult to present the bait properly. After a couple of matches, despite catching lower double figure weights I was lying nowhere in the league having had a few good batterings from anglers who had consistently caught 16 to 20 lbs to be well up in their sections. I decided to have a word with Bob Nudd who was doing well in the league and from whom I had learnt such a lot about pole fishing over the last few years. Upon his advice I decided to switch my tactics and to fish groundbait with caster, hemp and joker mixed in and bloodworm or caster on the hook, more in line with going for skimmers than the roach which had been my previous target species. I fished the next match and drew peg 80, and despite a strong wind I won the match with 25 lbs of roach and skimmers. I found that I could catch well on the bloodworm but due to the wind I was unable to present the caster properly. On those occasions when the wind dropped and I could present the caster right by leaving it in a few seconds longer and holding everything tight, I did catch fish two or three ounces bigger than those I was catching on the bloodworm. But mainly I had to use the bloodworm due to the conditions.

Anyway, the last match came and I had moved up the placings a good bit and providing I could get a reasonable result I stood a chance of getting in to the lower end of the prize list. I drew next but one to Bob Nudd, with Bob being on the end peg. It was a good area, in the 80's and I knew it was going to be a cracking match. We had a feeder man between us so Bob had got a golden chance to win the match and sew up the league. Again it was really windy and the longest length of pole I could comfortably hold was 9 metres so I plumbed the depth on the 9 metre line, sitting as far out in the water as possible on my platform and it was about 3½ ft deep. I had mixed my groundbait up the night before to make sure it was thoroughly and evenly soaked to the right consistency and it was just a basic 50–50 of brown crumb and Sensas Magic. Into this I put in my hemp, casters and jokers with a few bloodworm and when the whistle went I introduced 8 good balls into the 9 metre line and started off by fishing a .75 gramme float with a size 20 hook tied to a 1 lb bottom, with an olivette about 12 in from the hook and a couple of No 10 droppers which I moved about or bunched together as required. For the hookbait I used either a double bloodworm or bloodworm and caster, or on occasions just a single caster on the hook depending upon the strength of the wind. I also had a lighter strung out rig

and a heavier olivette rig set up on spare top sections to alternate with
as and when the wind strength dictated it. When the wind eased I went
on to the caster, as once again this was producing a better stamp of
fish of 6 or 7 ozs as opposed to 3 or 4 ozs on the bloodworm, and I
could catch them just as quickly, as they were taking the bait on the
drop just the same.

After the initial eight balls I was introducing a smaller, softer ball
every three or four casts and I started catching roach slowly but steadily
as was Bob on the next but one peg. I was hoping for a few bream
to move in but at 9 metres it was that much shallower than on the 12
metre line and they would just not move in. Halfway through the match
we were both neck and neck and the catch rate had speeded up and
the size of roach was slowly beginning to increase. With two hours of
the match to go I was caning them but Bob was absolutely murdering
them and he was gradually beginning to pull ahead. He had switched
to loose feeding with maggot by this time and had switched to a light
strung out rig, taking them on the drop.

In the last 1½ hours the wind began to ease and I was able to use
the caster more and more and I was catching as many as Bob but they
were each a couple of ounces heavier. Dick Clegg came and sat behind
me and I said 'Bob's murdering them'. After about 20 minutes of watching
us both Dick said 'I reckon you have caught about 3½ lbs to Bob's
2½ lbs'. This was very encouraging as it gave me a chance of pulling
back his early lead. Fortunately it was a day when everything went reasonably well. Despite the wind I did not get into any tangles and I had
dropped very few fish off of the hook as can often happen when you
are swinging or skimming in fish of that size to hand.

After the whistle went for the end of the match I asked Bob what
he thought he had caught, and with his usual accuracy he said about
21 to 22 lbs. I thought 'Well, I must also have something like that' and
I knew it was going to be close.

At the weigh in Bob's catch weighed 22 lbs 2 ozs and I just pipped
him with 22 lbs 10 ozs. It certainly opened my eyes to the potential of
bloodworm and joker to catch bigger fish when they are present. It is
not just a small fish bait as many people imagine.

Q. Don: One match I remember well was one of my first successes
using the pole on flowing water. It was a Steve Toone Long Higgin Saturday match and on the day the river was in perfect condition. I drew
peg number 8 next to a well known angler in this area and I knew exactly
what he was going to do—fish the feeder on the wasp grub. I never even
set my pole up at the beginning of the match as I knew peg 8 and I
decided to fish the stickfloat and the bomb.

I started off on the stickfloat and caught a few little roach and gudgeon but I was missing a lot of bites, and the other angler was catching these 10 oz to 1 lb chub every cast in and after an hour he was 10 lb up on me and I had only got just over a pound in my net. I thought to myself, 'well, this is no good' and all of these missed bites were haunting me so I decided to drop everying and rig up the pole, as I was doing no good with the running line and I had nothing to loose. I had only just got this Shakespeare carbon pole, and at that time the pole was seldom used on the Trent, we were still in the experimental stage and all the matches were being won on either the stickfloat or the feeder.

I set the pole up 7 metres to hand with a .75 gramme float. I used 2 No 8 plus 4 No 6 droppers strung out, with 3 No 6 bunched two-fifths of the way up the line. The hook was a size 20 to ¾ lb hooklength with bronze maggot on the hook. I plumbed the depth, trimmed up the float and on the very first run down the float dipped and I landed a 10 oz roach. In the next half an hour I really started to batter the roach, on the drop and running just down the peg, then gradually they went off and I lost them. Fortunately as the roach went off a shoal of skimmers moved in and I started to catch these 8 to 10 oz skimmers.

After a while these went off but then I caught a chub of about 2 lb, and all the time this was going on the other angler was still catching his chub, but they were also beginning to slow down.

After I caught my 2 lb chub everything went dead so I picked up my leger rod and dropped it in just past where I caught it and got another chub about ¾ lb, then again everything went dead. I had still been constantly feeding the 7 metre line and when I picked up the pole again the roach had come back. The other angler was still catching chub and I estimated that he was in front of me by at least 5 lbs. Fortunately these roach kept coming until the last hour when again things started to slow down. Again I alternated between the bomb and the pole and by now the other angler had also stopped catching. In the last ten minutes I decided to persevere on the pole, but with double maggot on the hook in the hope of attracting a bigger fish. With 5 minutes to go my gamble paid off and I hooked and landed a chub of about 2½ lbs.

At the weigh in I won the match with 25 lbs and the other angler came second with 23 lbs so that last bonus chub had won me the match. After this experience I put a lot more effort into refining the pole techniques on the rivers and on suitable venues it began to play an increasing role in my overall match plans.

These days Long Higgin is now a regular pole venue during the summer months, due to it being so deep and slow and it is seldom you ever see a rod and reel set up on an open match at this time of year.

BEWARE

OVERHEAD ELECTRIC POWER LINES

WARNING!

Living for fishing is one thing. Dying for it, or maiming yourself for life, is quite another. The one blot on the history and development of pole fishing in the last decade has been the number of serious accidents involving poles and overhead power lines.

The new carbon poles are frighteningly efficient at conducting electricity. They are long enough nowadays to make contact with power lines, but they do not even need to connect. Get one near enough and the power arcs across, with devastating results.

Fellow anglers have been killed. Two friends of ours have been horribly burned, and one has lost part of a leg. It should never have happened; it cannot happen to you or to us? But of course it can, unless you and we take the greatest of care.

So obey warning notices, and the advice from the electricity generating industry and the National Federation of Anglers to LOOK OUT and LOOK UP whenever you even think about setting up pole tackle in an area you are not familiar with.

Perhaps the reason why "lightning" never strikes twice is that it does not usually have to....

PLEASE DON'T DIE FOR YOUR FISHING!